PROPHETS
&
THEIR
BURDENS

I0142127

EMMANUEL BABA-LOLA

Prophets and Their Burdens

Copyright © 2022 Emmanuel Baba-Lola

All Rights Reserved. No part of this publication may be translated, reproduced, or transmitted in any form or by any means, electronic or mechanical, including photocopying, recording, or any information storage and retrieval system, without the written permission of the publisher.

Unless otherwise stated, all Scripture verses are taken from the New King James Version of the Bible © Thomas Nelson, Inc.

Scripture quotations marked KJV are from King James; NIV, New International Version; GNB, Good News Bible; NASV, New American Standard Version translations of the Holy Bible.

Published by

MISSIONS AID NETWORK

© Rabboni Books

Website: www.acts1038.com

Email: tell@acts1038.com

Tel: +1-507-405-2117 (USA)

ISBN: 978-1-907644-09-2

Printed in the USA, 2022

DEDICATION

To Dr. Isaac O. Crown of the Peculiar People's Church For all nations who believed in me when only a few people do and consecrated me a Reverend Gentleman, October 31, 1990. Thank you for your vision! Your prophecies are accurate and have come true! Love you loads.

Table of Contents

ACKNOWLEDGMENTS

This book is released to celebrate the Lord's grace and tender mercies on my life for the past thirty years of ordination as a Reverend Gentleman.

Therefore, I am very grateful to the Lord and those who believed in me when I was little. I am very thankful to many people who supported us and embraced our ministries over the years. I am grateful to the ministers and members of the New Wine Assembly, Lagos; you were with me when support was critical.

From the board of Missions Aid Network to the members of Ireland's Prophetic Prayer Conference (PPC) planning committee to every minister and participant in our conferences in the Republic of Ireland, I am grateful for your service to our God, your love, support, and friendship.

A big thank you to all my people in the USA, from the board members of Missions Aid Network in Maryland to the members and friends of our Faith Clinic, Rochester, MN, to every minister who associates with and patronizes our ministries.

I am blessed to marry my wife, Grace. Words fail

when it comes to my appreciation of your love and loyalty. I am speechless! Thank you. My children bore the brunt of our ministries as I travel often and struggled to find time for them when at home. I love you to pieces! You don't even have an idea.

Thank you to everyone who opposes our ministries and fought the grace and mercies of God that we enjoy. You helped me to discover myself and made me strong. I bless the Lord for you too.

Rochester, MN
October 31, 2022.

PREFACE

The most controversial ministry gift, by a wide margin, is the prophet—both in the Old and New Testaments, including today. A Prophet is controversial by default because as God's minister for special duties, He speaks the mind of God, who said:

> *"For My thoughts are not your thoughts, Nor are your ways My ways," says the Lord. "For as the heavens are higher than the earth, So are My ways higher than your ways, And My thoughts than your thoughts (Isa. 55: 8-9, NKJV).*

The only way to relate to the Lord, whose thoughts and ways are much different and higher than ours and who has no maximum in His qualities, is to submit to Him. Since two cannot walk together except they agree (Amos 3:3), it is incumbent on us to always agree with the Lord—something the human race has found challenging to do, perhaps because we are set in our ways.

Secondly, a Prophet is controversial by default because there are two parts to spiritual guidance:

> *For we know in part and we prophesy in part. 10 But when that which is perfect has come, then that*

which is in part will be done away (1Cor. 13: 9-10, NKJV).

So, there is the knowledge part and the prophecy part. A look into the Holy Bible shows that knowledge is where prophecy fails, and prophecy is where knowledge fails. Take the parents of Samson as an example:

> *Then his father and mother said to him, "Is there no woman among the daughters of your brethren, or among all my people, that you must go and get a wife from the uncircumcised Philistines?" And Samson said to his father, "Get her for me, for she pleases me well." But his father and mother did not know that it was of the Lord—that He was seeking an occasion to move against the Philistines. For at that time the Philistines had dominion over Israel (Jud. 14: 3-4, NKJV).*

The above is how the parents of Samson took a righteous position in ignorance of the prophetic. God had said that the Israelites must not intermarry with their surrounding nation because they would lure them to serve their no-gods. However, God has the plan to make the Philistines clash with Samson to pave the ways for Israel's deliverance from their oppressors.

> *Where there is no revelation, people cast off restraint; but blessed is the one who heeds wisdom's instruction (Pro. 29: 18, NIV).*

Revelation imparts wisdom and readiness. The enemy can take you by surprise when you don't have it.

Knowledge is so crucial to spirituality that God lamented that His people, despite all blessings, prophecies, and heritage, perish for lack of knowledge (Hos. 4:6). Josiah died in battle, contrary to the prophecy that he would die in peace. Saul, Jehu, Jeroboam, etc., wasted prophecies and promises about them and missed their destinies because they rejected knowledge. I wish the Chief Baker had known that the God of Joseph is a deliverer and asked for His help! He would have escaped execution.

To make matters worse for a ministry that attracts controversy, we have some fringe elements in the prophet communities. Among the Churches, we also have teachers inspired by the enemy to disclaim the ministries of prophets and apostles and deny prophecies and allied gifts of the Holy Spirit. I am writing this piece to let Believers know the great blessings of the most regulated ministry gift in the Holy Bible.

I have studied the arguments of the cessationists who deny the gifts of the Spirit: prophecy, tongues, healing, miracles, and the ministry gifts of the Apostles and Prophets. They are deliberate in their denials because they use too many maneuverings and insincerity to be ignorant of what they are doing. Fraud is involved when simple things become rocket science for brilliant people. They are just too arrogant to agree with the Lord on the gifts of the Spirit and thus suppress the truth in their unrighteousness (Rom. 1: 18). I employ you to observe how they have edited our Holy Scriptures as exposed in this book.

1

Has Prophecy Ceased?

We have folks in the church, aptly described as "cessationists," who teach that the gifts of the Holy Spirit have ceased, including the gift of prophecy and the ministry gifts of the Apostles and Prophets.

My purpose is not to reason with them but with those who have not taken their leaven because they have made up their minds. From my experiences with some of them, even if you successfully prove them wrong by the Scriptures, they will not yield. This is because their doctrines have become how they identify.

Therefore, no matter the evidence, they are blinded by ego, resentment, and hatred and have deliberately lost the capacity to learn otherwise.

In 2019, an elderly Pastor (not a Cessationist) well respected by my family visited me in the office. He explained that you must belong to a "click" (movement) in the Body of Christ. He said that the main requirement is to believe the movement's doctrines. He recently moved from one movement to another, and when he gave me an example of what they believe, that a Christian cannot be possessed by a demon, I retorted, "but I can give you an example of that in the Holy Bible." His reaction was shocking to me till now: he threw both his hands at me and said, "Please, don't tell me. I don't want to change my mind." I'd wanted to tell him of Simon, the sorcerer; he gave his life to Christ under the ministry of Phillip the Evangelist, burnt all his charms, and got baptized. However, according to Apostle Peter, he was poisoned by bitterness and bound by iniquity—demons (Acts 8: 9-24).

This is how territorial powerful men and women have divided the Body of Christ and drawn disciples after themselves who will have little or nothing to do with Believers outside their click.

They are brazen about their claims and will have nothing to do with those of us who rightly hold the opposing view. I was once invited to minister at a conference in Wisconsin, United States, where the choir of a cessationist church was invited to minister. They, however, pulled out barely one week before the program when they learned that I run a Prophetic ministry because they cannot even worship God with anyone who believes in the gifts of the Holy Spirit. Of course, Pastor John McArthur Jr. has reportedly said in one of his messages that those who believe in the gifts of the Holy Spirit are not part of the Body of Christ! That is not surprising from a man who built a volcanic doctrine on sentiments, insinuations, history, deliberate wrong definitions, and outright misinformation.

These folks will use just anything to smear those who believe the Holy Scriptures, and some among us who believe Scriptures on the gifts of the Holy Spirit, incredibly a few but prominent Charismatics, don't help matters sometimes, by their goofy doctrines and fringe practices. However, the Scripture enjoins us to contend for the faith.

> *Beloved, while I was very diligent to write to you concerning our common salvation, I found it necessary to write to you exhorting you to contend earnestly for the faith which was once for all delivered to the saints (Jude 3, NKJV).*

We cannot just ignore them to do our ministry but must expose them to protect the young in faith from their leaven.

Of course, they are very brazen and voracious in their attacks on us who believe. I watched a video where a cessationist compared a laughing hysteria in

Reverend Kenneth E. Hagin's meeting to similar laughter in a Hindu gathering and then declared that what happened in Hagin's ministry was Kundalini spirit.

So, in a similarity between God's kingdom and the devil's, these people give originality to Satan (even though he is the counterfeiter), forgetting that in the Bible times, there were God's prophets and Satan's prophets; we have prophecies from God's prophets and the prophets & prophetesses of Baal. So, by the same token, all prophecies must be by the spirit of Baal!

Further, they ridicule us on the episodes of falling under the power, and many believe that it is demonic and that where you find it in the Holy Bible, it is an act of judgment. Again, they deliberately ignore that John fell under the power before Christ (Rev. 1: 17) and that Peter, James, and John fell under the power on the Mountain of Transfiguration (Matt. 17: 1-8).

The incredible thing is that their bases, championed by Pastor John McArthur Jr., author of "The Charismatic chaos" and "Strange fire," are entirely extrabiblical. These they do by making spurious claims and the deliberate use of formulated definitions, wrong purpose of prophecies and miracles, and other gifts of the Spirit of God, including the ministry gifts of the Apostles and Prophets. In a nutshell, this is a doctrine of demons that Apostle Paul talked about in these last days. I will take "The Charismatic chaos" as a study case to illustrate how ridiculous their claims are.

The people who know that the Holy Scriptures are inspired by the Holy Spirit and study it reverently have nothing to worry about. I gave my life to Christ on my sixteenth birthday, and Bible study aids were not available to me, so I made it a habit of reading the Bible, word by word and line by line, yearly. I still have some of those Bibles where every page was heavily highlighted. I am enamored by the ability of Bible writers to communicate very effectively.

The visions of the Prophets were photographic; imagine the visions of Daniel, of goats with two heads and many horns representing something or somebody. God has immortalized vital messages in ways that cannot be corrupted or misunderstood over the ages! I noticed that nobody teaches better than Jesus Christ; He is a word painter that uses stories and parables to paint and cast images into the mind. Jesus always brings a concept to His teachings. No wonder, His affectionate name by His Disciples was Rabboni (Teacher) and not a Miracle worker.

So, very early in my walk with the Lord, I discovered the Bible is well written, well inspired, and so easy to understand that you only need a John McArthur to confuse you!

Extrabiblical Claims & Spurious Definitions

Regrettably, because he reads the Holy Bible with incurable unbelief in the gifts of the Spirit, John McArthur thinks 1Corinthians chapters 12-14 is a satire and treats it so. Now, look at 1Cor. 14: 1-5 and see how he imposed his unbelief forcefully on verses 2&4:

> *Pursue love, and desire spiritual gifts, but especially that you may prophesy. 2 For he who speaks in a tongue does not speak to men but to God, for no one understands him; however, in the spirit he speaks mysteries. 3 But he who prophesies speaks edification and exhortation and comfort to men. 4 He who speaks in a tongue edifies himself, but he who prophesies edifies the church. 5 I wish you all spoke with tongues, but even more that you prophesied; [a]for he who prophesies is greater than he who speaks with tongues, unless indeed he interprets, that the church may receive edification. (1Cor. 14:1-5 NKJV).*

MacArthur's comment on vs. 2 & 4: "he was using irony, pointing out the futility of speaking with tongues without an interpreter, because only God would know if anything was said" (page 228). Can you see what he has done here? The only way to justify his heresy is to change the genre of this passage to mean its opposite!

The word "irony" came from the Greek word,

"eironeia," which means "feigned ignorance." You therefore, cannot have an irony without the use of exaggerations or contradiction or sarcasm; none of which exists in the passage above. Instead, what you notice is Paul building up his points and explaining purpose and workability.

Not done, MacArthur added in the footnote, "Because of the absence of any definite article in the Greek text, it is also possible to translate this verse as, 'One who speaks in a tongue does not speak to men but to a god'—referring to a pagan deity" (page 228 n.17).

Meanwhile, Paul wished that they all spoke with tongues in Vs. 5 and ended this same chapter by saying:

> *Therefore, brethren, desire earnestly to prophesy, and do not forbid to speak with tongues. 40 Let all things be done decently and in order (1Cor. 14: 39-40, NKJV).*

So, McArthur, by implication, believes then that Paul possibly wished Corinthians to speak to a pagan deity and commanded them to not forbid speaking to a pagan god in the Church! This is proof positive that this passage is far from being an irony.

What is more illuminating is verses 18-19:

> *18 I thank my God I speak with tongues more than you all; 19 yet in the Church I would rather speak*

five words with my understanding, that I may teach others also, than ten thousand words in a tongue (1Cor. 14: 18, NKJV).

If verses 2 & 4 are ironic, as McArthur claims, what is Paul saying in Vs. 18 & 19? Did he speak to a pagan god and boast of it? Was he condemning speaking with tongues like McArthur claims he did in verses 2 & 4?

McArthur was simply rewriting that passage by changing its genre because the natural meaning of the passage is not hidden or difficult to understand. The only way the passage could be ironic is if the writing is satire, which it isn't. If this is not blaspheming, then I don't know what it means; and this is the guy that accuses others of disrespecting the Holy Scriptures!

Meanwhile, verse 14 above is the essence of what Paul said in this chapter, but McArthur saw an irony that plays well into his script of discrediting speaking with tongues. When it comes to pushing his false narratives, exegetical correctness doesn't matter. I can understand if unbelievers turn our Holy Scriptures into parodies; it is unfortunate when a believer goes to such a ridiculous extent to canonize a blatant lie.

Next is MacArthur's view of 1 Corinthians 13:8 instantly below:

Love never fails; but if there are gifts of prophecy, they will be done away; if there are tongues, they will cease; if there is knowledge, it will be done away. 9 For we know in part and we prophesy in part; 10 but when the perfect comes, the partial will be done away. 11 When I was a child, I used to speak like a child, think like a child, reason like a child; when I became a man, I did away with childish things. 12 For now we see in a mirror dimly, but then face to face; now I know in part, but then I will know fully just as I also have been fully known. 13 But now faith, hope, love, abide these three; but the greatest of these is love (NASB).

He claims that prophecy and knowledge will be done away "when the perfect comes," according to verse 10. The perfect is when we see the Lord "face to face" (vs. 12). However, he said, "the gift of tongues will 'stop itself'" (page 231 n.20), adding that "When is not stipulated, but they won't be around when the perfect thing arrives. History suggests that tongues ceased shortly after Paul wrote this epistle" (page 231).

It is evident that McArthur, without shame or respect, is screwing the Holy Word of God; the passage is not ambiguous, "done away" and "cease" have the same "face to face" statute of limitation.

By putting an expiry date on our Holy Scriptures, he has probably done what no one else has ever done in the history of the Church. Here, he just becomes ridiculous and maybe desperate. It is understandable when one says that some prophecies in the Scriptures have been fulfilled but putting an expiry date on passages that are not even prophecies is something else that is pure sacrilege. It is contemptuous to treat Scriptures like mere literature that can be subjected to personal and baseless interpretation.

If he was right on his expiry theory, how can we be sure that other writings of Paul have not expired, or why is that peculiar to his writings on the gifts of the Spirit? What about his writing on the fruit of the Spirit? Why has that not expired too? Which other writers have portions of their writings expired in the Scriptures, or why would that be peculiar to the writings of Paul alone?

The heresy is not farfetched; he holds down the truth in unrighteousness. John McArthur has become a living example of how unbelief can reduce a good person to ridiculous agitations. Irrespectively, the Holy Scriptures cannot be broken, altered, or set aside:

> *If he called them 'gods,' to whom the word of God came—and Scripture cannot be set aside (John 10:35, NIV).*

The Cessationists set Scriptures aside when they put the expiry date on the Scriptures that they disagree with.

In an unbridled effort to reassign the biblical purpose

of the gifts of the Spirit, McArthur took the liberty to divide the nine gifts of the Spirit in 1Cor. 12: 8-10 into two categories that suit his doctrine of denial: "temporary sign gifts" and "permanent edifying gifts" (page 1990), without any reference to the Holy Scriptures whatsoever.

In chapter 9, "Does God Heal?" he contends that "These were specific enablements (sic) given to certain believers for the purpose of authenticating or confirming God's Word when it was proclaimed in the early Church before the Scriptures were written. The temporary sign gifts included prophecy (revelatory prophecy), miracles, healings, tongues, and interpretation of tongues. The sign gifts had a unique purpose: to give the apostles credentials, that is, to let the people know that these men all spoke the truth of God. Once the Word of God was inscripturated, the sign gifts were no longer needed and they ceased" (page 199).

These "permanent edifying gifts" include "knowledge, wisdom, prophecy (authoritative preaching), teaching, exhortation, faith (or prayer), discernment, showing mercy, giving, administration, and helps" (page 199).

In his new list of current gifts in the Body of Christ, only five of the gifts in 1Cor. 12: 8-10, make the list in some ways: (word of) wisdom, (word of) knowledge, faith, and discerning of spirits. The fifth gift, prophecy, has been whittled down to "authoritative preaching" (or "the ability to proclaim truth powerfully" (page 231), as "revelatory prophecy" was temporary and has expired.

On all other gifts, like the gifts of healing, he said with finality that "those who claim the gift of healing do not really have it" (page 203), insisting that the gifts served their purpose and were withdrawn by God.

MacArthur's explanation for the cessation of the "sign gifts" is mind bugling: these gifts exist to authenticate the gospel before the Word of God was "inscripturated;" and, secondly, to certify genuine apostleship until the Scriptures were completed. However, the Bible clearly states that spiritual gifts are manifestations of the Holy Spirit, not apostolic credentials. Further, how come ordinary Church members manifested these gifts since the purpose was not about them at all? Why is it that Paul or any other Apostle did not give any information at all on such a very important statute of limitation about the gifts?

Pastor John McArthur wrongly teaches that the idea of these gifts being in operation today means that there are new revelations and that the Holy Bible is incomplete.

Please, notice his deliberate use of false definition to lubricate his aim; it is intentional because there is nowhere in the Scriptures that supports his portrayal of the purpose of prophecy or the division of it into "revelatory prophecy" and "authoritative preaching." The word "Prophecy" means "to foretell," and what is correct to say is that prophecies are Scriptures and not what helped authenticate the writers of Scriptures.

Meanwhile, the Scriptures do not leave us in doubt about the purpose of prophecy:

> *But he who prophesies speaks edification and exhortation and comfort to men. 4 He who speaks in a tongue edifies himself, but he who prophesies edifies the Church. I wish you all spoke with tongues, but even more that you prophesied; for he who prophesies is greater than he who speaks with tongues, unless indeed he interprets, that the Church may receive edification. (1 Cor. 14: 3-5, NKJV)*

> *Therefore if the whole Church comes together in one place, and all speak with tongues, and there come in those who are uninformed or unbelievers, will they not say that you are out of your mind? But if all prophesy, and an unbeliever or an uninformed person comes in, he is convinced by all, he is convicted by all. nd thus the secrets of his heart are revealed; and so, falling down on his face, he will worship God and report that God is truly among you (1 Cor. 14: 23-25, NKJV).*

Paul, a conscientious and meticulous teacher of the Word, spelled out the purpose of prophecies in the above passage: edification, the exhortation of members of the Church, and the winning of unbelievers to Christ. He said further:

A spiritual gift is given to each of us so we can help each other (1Cor. 12: 7, NLV).

Look at the language, "A spiritual gift is given to each of us so we can...." Again, we see the edification of the Believers, in other words, as a purpose of prophecy; some translations use the phrase "for the common good" or "for profit."

Do not neglect the gift that is in you, which was given to you by prophecy with the laying on of the hands of the eldership (1Tim. 4: 14, NKJV).

Yet again, we see another purpose of prophecy in this Scripture: impartation of spiritual gifts.

Apart from the purpose clearly written, we also see what the prophets did with their prophecies in the Holy Bible by helping them in various ways (Ezra 5:2).

MacArthur went further: "Nothing in Scripture indicates that the miracles of the apostolic age were meant to be continuous in subsequent ages" (page 117). He writes: "Miracles were unique to the apostles and those who worked most closely with them" (pages 120-21). Still, MacArthur adds that, "The average Christian had no ability to perform signs and wonders" (page 121).

Well, he is shifting the pole here because if miracles were unique to the Apostles, how could those who worked with them perform miracles? He probably thinks that we are dumb. Imagine the claim, "no miracles ever occurred in the entire New Testament record except in the presence of an apostle or one directly commissioned by an apostle," adding that "the power never went any further" (page 121).

Seriously? What about the following passages that destroy his argument?

> *After this the Lord appointed seventy-two others and sent them two by two ahead of him to every town and place where he was about to go... The seventy-two returned with joy and said, "Lord, even the demons submit to us in your name." He replied, "I saw Satan fall like lightning from heaven. 19 I have given you authority to trample on snakes and scorpions and to overcome all the power of the enemy; nothing will harm you (Luke 10: 1, 17-19, NIV).*

Those were seventy-two other disciples that were not part of the Apostles, and Jesus sent them out and performed miracles. Moreover, the Lord gave them the authority to trample Satan without repercussions!

> *Is anyone among you sick? Let them call the elders*

of the Church to pray over them and anoint them with oil in the name of the Lord. And the prayer offered in faith will make the sick person well; the Lord will raise them up. If they have sinned, they will be forgiven. Therefore confess your sins to each other and pray for each other so that you may be healed. The prayer of a righteous person is powerful and effective (James 5: 14-16, NIV).

The above passage was not written by an Apostle but by James, the brother of Christ and Bishop of Jerusalem. He asked elders to anoint and pray for the sick for their healing. That obviously counters McArthur's claim that miracles only happen by the Apostles or in their presence.

"Teacher," said John, "we saw someone driving out demons in your name and we told him to stop, because he was not one of us."

"Do not stop him," Jesus said. "For no one who does a miracle in my name can in the next moment say anything bad about me, 40 for whoever is not against us is for us (Mark 9: 38-39).

This is it! Right from the mouth of the Savior Himself!! You don't have to be an Apostle of Christ to do miracles in His name. You only must believe in the Messiah.

Further, McArthur edited Mark 16:17-18 to say something completely different. Please, look at the passage:

> *And these signs will follow those who believe: In My name they will cast out demons; they will speak with new tongues; they will take up serpents; and if they drink anything deadly, it will by no means hurt them; they will lay hands on the sick, and they will recover." Mark 16:17-18 (NKJV)*

MacArthur states: "It is incorrect to assert that these signs should be the norm for all believers today" (page 102).

Sadly, he did not even spare the Words directly spoken by the Messiah; his insinuations amended the Words of our Beloved Savior, and the treachery here is blatant. Our Lord said, "those who believe," but McArthur said that could only refer to the Apostles. So, it's either that only the Apostles can believe or that those who believe among them, meaning that some of them may disbelieve the Savior.

History says that the scribes who copied the Holy Scriptures paused to change the pen or clean it before and after they wrote the name of God. Such was the respect and holy reference they had. So, how can a pastor take the liberty to force his insinuations on the Word of the only Begotten Son of God, thereby changing its genre and meaning and calling it an interpretation of the Scripture?

He falsely affirms that believers, in general, have not

demonstrated these signs in history because "these signs were true of one certain group—the apostolic community" (page 102). In fact, he said, "if the Bible is not convincing that tongues will shortly stop, history is!"

MacArthur accuses the Charismatics of basing their doctrines on experience instead of the Word of God. However, in a twist, he relies on his contrived historical evidence that tongues ceased shortly after Paul's letter when he said, "If the Bible is not convincing that tongues will shortly stop, history is."

However, history is not on his side either, and we have a lot of historical evidence that McArthur would like to bury. Church fathers like Justin Martyr (100-165 A.D.), Irenaeus (140-203 A.D.), Tertullian (160/170-215/220 A.D.), Augustine (354-430 A.D.), etc., all affirmed miracles. Martin Luther (1483-1546 A.D.) believed in prophecy. It is beyond the scope of this book to delve into history to expose the lie of McArthur. I will refer you to a great work that already detailed the move of the Holy Spirit in terms of miracles and all other gifts of the Spirit: "Miracles And Manifestations of the Holy Spirit in the History of the Church" by Jeff Doles.

McArthur quotes 2Cor. 12:12 to buttress his view that some gifts were limited to the Apostles. However, there is nothing ambiguous about the passage to elicit debate except that he seems to believe it is irony again:

"The signs of a true apostle were performed among you in all patience, with signs and wonders and mighty works" (RSV).

His comment: "If doing miracles had been the common experience of ordinary Christians, it would be foolish for Paul to try to prove his apostleship by citing the miracles he had done" (page 121).

However, verse 28 of the same chapter states:

"God has appointed in the church first apostles, second prophets, third teachers, then workers of miracles" (RSV).

Here "workers of miracles" are clearly separate from the Apostles. As I've said before, the Holy Bible is so easy to understand that you only need a John McArthur to confuse you!

Therefore, no one can talk like an oracle that miracles have an onerous purpose of writing the Scriptures.

So, what is his reference other than unbelief insinuations? If he is right, with the many instances of prophecies in the New Testament by Believers in different churches and locations, how is it that only a few people wrote scriptures? How is it that only a few Apostles of Christ wrote scriptures? Why did Church members who neither needed presumed authentication nor write Scriptures prophesy? We have nine authors in the New Testament:

1. Matthew, one of the twelve Disciples of the Lord.

2. Mark, his full name is John Mark, son of Mary (Acts 12: 12) and cousin of Barnabas (Col. 4: 10). He was a Disciple of Apostle Peter whose short work with Paul and Barnabas led to their split. He later reunited with Paul (2Tim. 4: 11).

3. Luke, the physician author of Luke and Acts. He was a close Disciple of Apostle Paul and the only Gentile author of the New Testament.

4. John, one of the twelve Disciples of Christ and author of John, the three letters of John, and Revelation.

5. Paul, the Apostle, authored thirteen out of the twenty-seven books of the New Testament.

6. James, brother of Christ (Matt. 13: 55) and author of James.

7. Peter, one of the twelve Disciples of Christ and author of the two letters of Peter.

8. Jude, brother of Christ (Acts 1: 14) and author of Jude.

9. Hebrews, Author unknown. He had an excellent knowledge of the Old Testament and was a great writer of Greek. The early Church father, Origen, said in 200 A.D. about the author of Hebrews, "Only God knows!"

As you can see, only four of the twelve Apostles wrote

Scriptures, making it five, if the unknown writer of Hebrews was another one of them. McArthur's claim that miracles, prophecies, and tongues were given to authenticate the Apostles and Prophets for writing Scriptures fell apart!

A look into the Scriptures shows clearly that all Scriptures, Old and New Testaments, came by inspiration:

> *All Scripture is given by inspiration of God, and is profitable for doctrine, for reproof, for correction, for instruction in righteousness, 17 that the man of God may be complete, thoroughly equipped for every good work (2 Tim. 3: 16, NKJV).*

We have different types of books in the Holy Bible: The Pentateuch (Law of Moses) like Exodus & Leviticus; Wisdom books like Proverbs & Ecclesiastics; Songs like Psalms & Songs of Solomon; Historical books like Kings, Chronicles, & Acts of the Apostles; Epistles (Letters) like the books of Corinthians, Jude, & Peter; Prophecy like Isaiah, Daniel & Revelation.

The passage above says all Scriptures were written by inspiration. However, most of these books were not written by the Prophets or the Apostles. So, the Book of Acts, written by Dr. Luke, is a product of the inspiration of God as the Book of Isaiah.

Furthermore, the writers of the Old Testament books

were not authenticated by miracles, prophecies, or tongues; why was that peculiar to the New Testament? Speaking with tongues, for example, is the signature gift of the New Testament, as no one ever spoke with tongues in the Old Testament. Yet, McArthur talks with finality on issues bigger than him that he disbelieves and fails to grasp.

The cessationists use extrapolations and wrong definitions to justify their claim that the offices of the Apostles and Prophets are already proscribed. For example, they extrapolated that since the Apostles saw Jesus Christ physically, an Apostle must see Jesus Christ openly like Apostle Paul, which they believe is no longer possible; therefore, there are no more Apostles. Further, the Apostles and Prophets were allegedly just to write Scriptures, and they are no more.

This is their stock-in-trade; they deliberately use wrong definitions to build their doctrine. There is nowhere in the Scriptures that describes the purpose of the Apostles and Prophets as writing the Scriptures. It is also evident that not only the Apostles wrote the New Testament; Dr. Luke, a disciple of Paul who wrote the Books of Luke and the Acts of the Apostles, was not an Apostle, and there is no record that he performed any miracle. The attitude here is apparent; they are right because they said so.

Notwithstanding, the Holy Scriptures clearly spelled out the purpose of an Apostle (a sent one) and that of

Prophets:

> *And He Himself gave some to be apostles, some prophets, some evangelists, and some pastors and teachers, 12 for the equipping of the saints for the work of ministry, for the edifying of the body of Christ, 13 till we all come to the unity of the faith and of the knowledge of the Son of God, to a perfect man, to the measure of the stature of the fullness of Christ; 14 that we should no longer be children, tossed to and fro and carried about with every wind of doctrine, by the trickery of men, in the cunning craftiness of deceitful plotting, 15 but, speaking the truth in love, may grow up in all things into Him who is the head—Christ— 16 from whom the whole body, joined and knit together by what every joint supplies, according to the effective working by which every part does its share, causes growth of the body for the edifying of itself in love (Eph. 4: 11-16, NKJV).*

In the above passage, the common purpose of the so-called five-fold ministries is not only stated, but their duration or statute of limitation was also clearly defined. Anyone claiming that the offices of the Apostles and Prophets have ended is a deliberate repudiation of the Holy Scriptures.

Apostles and Prophets are much needed today. An Apostle means "a sent one," a complete package and machine of the Gospel of Christ. He has been likened to the thumb, the only finger that can touch every other finger. He is a Prophet, Pastor, Evangelist, and Teacher. While the functions of the Old Testament and the New Testament Prophets are different in scope, a study of their ministries in the Bible clearly shows that a Prophet is a teacher that points the people in the right direction through prophecy and other prophetic gifts. When a Prophet is not a teacher, he is a Seer.

Meanwhile, Paul was not the first to write about the gifts of the Holy Spirit that we have in the New Testament; Prophet Joel, centuries before Paul, prophesied:

> *"And it shall come to pass afterward That I will pour out My Spirit on all flesh; Your sons and your daughters shall prophesy, Your old men shall dream dreams, Your young men shall see visions. And also on My menservants and on My maidservants I will pour out My Spirit in those days (Joel 2: 28-29, NKJV).*

Again, the purpose of outpouring the Spirit of God cannot be misunderstood, and it is not to authenticate the writers of the Scriptures. Paul wasn't a messianic figure, and according to his writings, some Christians of his day challenged his apostleship. The cessationists unwittingly and perhaps inadvertently idolized him to prove a wrong point.

Though Paul worked more than any other apostle, the Churches he did not plant were far more than the ones he founded. For example, Paul was said to have founded about twenty Churches directly or indirectly. We have evidence that these churches, like the other local churches, expanded by planting several other churches. So, he never spoke to the majority or could have spoken to all the Churches of his time. Therefore, how could the gifts of the Spirit stop when he stopped writing about them?

New Testament writings were Scriptures as soon as he wrote them by God's inspiration, and we have evidence to back it up. In 2 Peter 3:16, Peter declares Paul's epistles as Scriptures:

He writes the same way in all his letters, speaking in them of these matters. His letters contain some things that are hard to understand, which ignorant and unstable people distort, as they do the other Scriptures, to their own destruction (NIV).

Notice that he ranked Paul's writings with "the other scriptures." "Graphē," translated here as "Scriptures," occurs fifty-one times in the New Testament and refers to the Old Testament Scriptures every time.

Further, Paul categorized Luke's Gospel as "Scripture:"

For the Scripture says, "You shall not muzzle an ox while it treads out the grain," and, "The laborer is worthy of his wages." (1 Tim. 5:18, NKJV).

Not to muzzle an ox is quoted from Deut. 25: 4. However, "The laborer *is* worthy of his wages," only exists in the Book of Luke 10: 7. Paul refers to it as "Scripture."

Of course, these new Scriptures would take time to spread and reach most churches. The common practice was to use witnesses—those who heard Jesus Christ or the Apostles directly. After all these witnesses were gone, the Church fathers collated the Apostles' writings and that of their associates as our Scriptures in the New Testament. So, McArthur's claim that new Scriptures wait to be "Inscripturated" isn't valid.

It is noteworthy that when McArthur was asked in a video to give at least one Scriptural verse that supports his Cessationist claim. The only Scripture he quoted without mentioning the verse, he couldn't quote it correctly when he simply said, "The Bible says that the Apostles and the prophets are the foundations of the Church." The following is the verse in its context:

> *Now, therefore, you are no longer strangers and foreigners, but fellow citizens with the saints and members of the household of God, having been built on the foundation of the apostles and prophets, Jesus Christ Himself being the chief cornerstone, in whom the whole building, being fitted together, grows into a holy temple in the Lord, in whom you also are being built together for a dwelling place of*

God in the Spirit (Eph. 2: 19-22, NKJV).

Please, notice that it says, "the foundation of the apostles and prophets" and not that the Apostles were the foundation themselves. In addition, let's compare this to another passage:

> *According to the grace of God which was given to me, as a wise master builder I have laid the foundation, and another builds on it. But let each one take heed how he builds on it. For no other foundation can anyone lay than that which is laid, which is Jesus Christ (1Cor. 3: 10-11, NKJV).*

So, it is a fact that our Lord Jesus Christ is the foundation of the Church and not the Apostles. Sadly, this is the only verse that John McArthur can mention to justify a massive doctrine of his that has divided the Church. Even if the Apostles were the foundation, how did that justify the teaching that some gifts of the Holy Spirit have ceased? This is pure fishing for a passage that isn't there and proof positive that the Cessationists' claims are fickle, feeble, and extrabiblical.

He carries himself with such an air of self-righteous anger and authority that he talks like an oracle that needs not submit to the written Scripture by letting it explain itself.

One question destroys and exposes his claims as doctrines of demons: "How did he know that?"

because they are nowhere written in the Holy Bible. In claiming that there are no new revelations—which is true—he is giving a unique, new, private, but heretic revelation!

He and his ilk disrespect the Holy Scriptures by forcing their private opinions on the Scriptures and talking like oracles without any reference to them. Usually, misinterpretation of passages comes from interpretations out of context, ignorance of the Bible culture, understanding in light of one's culture, reading too much into parables and stories of the Holy Bible, cherry-picking of Scriptures, etc. However, they took the liberty to cancel Scripture passages as expired and force wrong meanings on others; when they do this much, they are not interpreting the Holy Scriptures but editing and rewriting the Holy Word of God. There is no way to read the Bible to know what they are saying.

How Did He know that?

The big question is how did he know that? How did he know that tongues stopped shortly after Paul wrote it? How did you know it's irony? How did you know that the gifts of prophecy are divided into two? How did you know that the gifts of prophecy and miracles were authenticators of the Apostles as writers of the scriptures? How did you know that that is their only purpose? How did you know that Apostles and prophets were to write scriptures and therefore have ceased? Where did you read that tongues are earthly languages and were not ecstatic even though they spoke as the Holy Spirit gave them utterance (Acts 2: 4)? There is no way to know those things from the passages of the Bible!

You have imposed these extra-biblical assumptions on our Holy Scriptures to edit them! These assumptions are very similar to the evolution theory, the only "science" whose evidence is fanciful assumptions that are academically justified by necessary presumptive assumptions. Like the evolution theory, the cessationists theory will never consider contrary evidence because it fears its veracity. Ignoring the truth does not confirm a lie, no matter how famously celebrated. The Lord will continue to bless His people who believe the Scriptures and surrender to Him. We believe and will continue to see God's glory and move wherever we go!

Every Believer must understand that leaders and followers are responsible for being truthful to the Word of God. To the leaders, the Scriptures admonish:

> *"But whoever causes one of these little ones who believe in Me to stumble, it would be better for him if a millstone were hung around his neck, and he were thrown into the sea (Mark 9: 42, NJKV).*

> *My brethren, let not many of you become teachers, knowing that we shall receive a stricter judgment.*

2 For we all stumble in many things. If anyone does not stumble in word, he is a perfect man, able also to bridle the whole body (James 3: 1, NKJV).

Therefore, it is dangerous for teachers of the Word of God to be so arrogant that they lock up their minds and refuse corrections. Like many others who identify by what they oppose, the cessationists will not take questions after their messages because they assume that it is impossible that they could be wrong. This is quite unlike our Lord Jesus Christ, who took to queries repeatedly from the Pharisees and other religious leaders of His time. If they are sincere, they will be open to questions and be ready to debate other Christians who question their interpretations of our Holy Scriptures. I take questions after my teachings everywhere I go because I am prepared to learn and do not want to mislead anyone. I have thus discovered the power of questions to demonstrate truth and expose errors. Only people with something to hide will avoid questions and disdain genuine opposing views. Apostle Paul commended those who verified his messages from the Holy Scriptures, and we are duty-bound to do the same as humble and sincere leaders:

As soon as it was night, the believers sent Paul and Silas away to Berea. On arriving there, they went to the Jewish synagogue. Now the Berean Jews were of more noble character than those in Thessalonica, for they received the message with great eagerness and examined the Scriptures every day to see if what Paul said was true (Acts 17: 10-

11, NKJV).

To the Followers, the Holy Bible Warns:

3 For the time will come when they will not endure sound doctrine, but according to their own desires, because they have itching ears, they will heap up for themselves teachers; 4 and they will turn their ears away from the truth, and be turned aside to fables. 5 But you be watchful in all things, endure afflictions, do the work of an evangelist, fulfill your ministry (2 Tim. 4: 3-5, NKJV).

Apostle Paul was putting the responsibility on the follower here. So, every follower is responsible for rejecting the "itching ears" syndrome that Paul warned about and desire to study the Bible themselves. It contradicts the Word of the Lord Himself to put ministers on a high pedestal and imbibe their teachings without vetting them.

8 But you, do not be called 'Rabbi'; for One is your Teacher, the Christ, and you are all brethren. 9 Do not call anyone on earth your father; for One is your Father, He who is in heaven. 10 And do not be called teachers; for One is your Teacher, the Christ. 11 But he who is greatest among you shall be your servant. 12 And whoever exalts himself will be humbled, and he who humbles himself will be exalted (Matt. 23: 8-12, NKJV).

Paul called Timothy "my son" in the Lord, and we know we have biological fathers. Jesus Christ did not deny those facts. However, He meant that God is our ultimate Father and Teacher that cannot be wrong. No human being is that big!

Biblical Purpose of Miracles

Meanwhile, the purpose of miracles is not far-fetched in the Holy Bible, and none of it is to validate any human being on earth. Miracles are about the name of Jesus and not any human personality. The purpose of miracles in Christ is aptly described in the book of Acts.

> *"Men of Israel, hear these words: Jesus of Nazareth, a Man attested by God to you by miracles, wonders, and signs which God did through Him in your midst, as you yourselves also know—(Acts 2: 22, NKJV)*

The number one purpose of miracles in the New Testament is to confirm no other person but the Messiah. Miracles are done in His name and because of Him (Acts 3: 12, 16). This is a fact of the New Testament. When John the Baptist sent his vitriolic message to the Savior, "Are you the one or shall we wait for another?" Jesus Christ validated Himself by His miracles and teachings:

> *4Jesus answered and said to them, "Go and tell John the things which you hear and see:5The blind*

see and the lame walk; the lepers are cleansed and the deaf hear; the dead are raised up and the poor have the gospel preached to them. 6And blessed is he who is not offended because of Me." (Matt. 11: 4-6, NKJV)

These are clearly written in Scriptures but when they disbelieve the Word of God, they also label those who believe it. For example, even though we believe that Jesus Christ is the healer and miracle worker, and that we are mere tools in His hand, thy call us "Faith healer."

The second purpose of miracles in the New Testament is God's mercy:

how God anointed Jesus of Nazareth with the Holy Spirit and with power, who went about doing good and healing all who were oppressed by the devil, for God was with Him (Acts 10: 38, NKJV).

To start with, hunger, sicknesses, and diseases are terrible traumas. People in severe pain often cannot listen to anything, including the Gospel of Christ. In my book, Let Me Run, I referenced a boy who responded to the missionaries preaching to him, "I am so hungry that I cannot hear what you're saying." We must ask ourselves why Christ usually solved physical problems like sicknesses before preaching to them.

In the history of world evangelism, helping people

has been a significant opportunity to preach the Gospel to the poor and lead them to Christ.

The Holy Bible is obvious on this:

> *4 Or do you despise the riches of His goodness, forbearance, and longsuffering, not knowing that the goodness of God leads you to repentance? (Rom 2: 4, NKJV)*

God's goodness leads people to repentance! Loving and helping people leads more people to God, by a wide margin, than scaring them up. It is a significant breakthrough when people personally experience God's love and reality.

When people live and enjoy plenty where there is safety, they can become entitled and behave callously towards the poor and needy. I have heard a popular televangelist Pastor in the USA preach that America should stop helping poor people in developing countries because their poverty is due to their government's stealing resources!

Further, the Lord's ministries on earth are comprised of Words and Deeds, described as doing good and setting people free.

> *The former account I made, O Theophilus, of all that Jesus began both to do and teach, (Acts 1: 1, NKJV)*

McArthur and many other cessationists live in an advanced world with too much food, good healthcare, and medications. So, they can easily sit in their comfortable homes and churches and teach that God does not heal or perform miracles again. How many of these denying folks have done mission work in areas of South America, Africa, the Caribbean, and Asia where there are no hospitals at all or even simple medication? Have they lived where even if these are available, it is beyond some people's reach financially? It is natural for all souls to call upon the Lord when in trouble, and to tell these helpless people that the Lord used to heal when the Scriptures were not complete but had stopped is not good news.

There is a reason the cessationists will never see miracles in their midst; it is called unbelief because, without faith, no one will see the glory of the Lord.

I have seen too many miracles and healings in our ministries and many others in very vulnerable parts of the world, where if God had not helped, the people would have been doomed to death. I had seen thousands of people come to Christ when they received or saw miracles. To the cessationists, those miracles are not from God, so will the devil deceive people to believe in Christ?

That a few people monetize the blood and sweat of Christ and profit from it is not a genuine reason to disdain the Lord's goodness and rescue for His people. Disbelieving the written Word of God because of some erroneous practices is self-righteousness and sin. We have similar stuff in Africa where some misguided elites claim that Christianity is a White man's religion because the slave traders were so-called Christians who baptized slaves and asked them to accept their fate as God-ordained. To them, abuse is definition or circumscription! It is a similar sentiment with the cessationists on the Gifts of the Spirit.

An Example of Biblical Prophecies Today

I want to give an example of a "revelatory" prophecy today that McArthur said no longer exists. This historical fact agrees perfectly with the Word of God and is vastly different from McArthur's allegation of building a doctrine on experience rather than the Word of God. If you have read this chapter from the bigging, you would have seen that the cessationists are guilty of their allegations as their doctrine lacks basis on the Word of God.

I am sharing this story because it is documented in a book available in both hard and soft copies by William Baker, "Proving God, proving Jesus." I was praying for people after our meeting in the "New Life Assembly of God Church, Reedsburg," Wisconsin, when a group of people entered the Church. I pointed to Bill (William Baker) to come forward for prayers and prophesied on him something like, "The Lord says that He heard how you denied His existence. You quoted Charles Darwin and Richard

Dawkins to convince yourself, but He asks me to tell you that He exists and wants to use you."

Unknown to me, Bill and his wife, now diseased, were visiting a family, John and Linda Chute, when everyone but Bill decided to come for my meeting. Since Bill went in a car with his wife, he had to come with them but quoted Darwin and Richard Dawkins in the vehicle that there is no God. He gave his life to Christ after that encounter.

Secondly, Bill attended another meeting where I ministered in Mauston, Wisconsin, hosted by Dr. Peggy and her husband, Scott Dennison. After my message, Bill was one of the people I called out for prayers. I gave him another prophecy that the Lord wants him to write a book on the existence of God. I described three chapters of the book and their topics. Unknown to me, God had instructed him to write the book, and he wrote three chapters but developed cold feet. He asked God to confirm through me that he must write the book before he left home—and the Lord did! Bill is on fire today for the Lord.

This is an example that McArthur says is only meant to authenticate the Apostles to write Scriptures and has been proscribed by God. Would the devil lead an atheist to Christ by revelatory prophecy? He has absolutely no Bible passage to back his false claim, while we believe the Holy Scriptures that it is not a satire and, therefore, the Lord is blessing us through His Holy Spirit. He has written a book of 416 pages,

"The Charismatic Chaos," in unbelief to discredit the gifts of the Spirit and the ministries of the Apostles and Prophets today. That is how difficult to deny the truth!

2

The Burden of Rejection

Lord, you coerced me into being a prophet, and I allowed you to do it. You overcame my resistance and prevailed over me. Now I have become a constant laughingstock. Everyone ridicules me. For whenever I prophesy, I must cry out, "Violence and destruction are coming!" This message from the Lord has made me an object of continual insults and derision. Sometimes I think, "I will make no mention of his message. I will not speak as his messenger anymore." But then his message becomes like a fire locked up inside of me, burning in my heart and soul. I grow weary of trying to hold it in; I cannot contain it.

I hear many whispering words of intrigue against me. Those who would cause me terror are everywhere! They are saying, "Come on, let's publicly denounce him!" All my so-called friends are just watching for something that would lead to my downfall. They say, "Perhaps he can be enticed into slipping up, so we can prevail over him and get our revenge on him." But the Lord is with me to help me like an awe-inspiring warrior. Therefore those who persecute me will fail and will not prevail over me. They will be thoroughly disgraced because they did not succeed. Their disgrace will never be forgotten (Jer. 20: 7-11, NET)

I f you have not read the Preface, please, go back there, as it is vital to understanding this chapter. When it comes to rejection and denial, no other ministry gift suffers like the prophets; not even close. Usually, it is the false prophets who tell people what they want to hear or scare them with lies that people celebrate; true prophets who say the mind of God are the ones that are rejected and even killed. You cannot be a people pleaser or politically correct if you stand in the prophetic ministry. How many prophets were loved by the people in the Holy Bible? How many were murdered? How many were not attacked at all?

The calling of the Prophet is not fun when people become rebellious to the Lord. When God's people who are supposed to follow Him turn against Him, who then is a Prophet to assume he will be accepted? The tricky part of the Prophet's job is that he often must correct the people and tell them what to do.

However, there are two words that all mankind dislike and struggle to keep: "Don't" and "Wait." For example, the Lord told Adam, "Don't" eat that fruit; we all know the story. Secondly, Jesus Christ told His Disciples to "Wait" and do nothing until the Holy Spirit came; however, they didn't wait, and barely a few days later, Peter stood up and led them to choose a replacement for Judas Iscariot. Who inspired him?

The Prophet is sent to speak for God in good and bad times. In bad times when people disobey the Lord, it becomes dangerous and could be fatal for the Prophet to speak for God. Let me bring it home. The current president of Nigeria, Mohammadu Buhari, is a known sympathizer of the Boko Haram Islamic terrorists who are predominantly members of his "Fulani" kinsmen. For example, these terrorists have killed several thousands of Christians in Northern Nigeria, wiping out many villages and churches in the most brutal ways, including burning people, including children alive, cutting people to pieces with machetes, etc. However, when these terrorists were arrested, Buhari decided to "Rehabilitate" them by spending millions of dollars on them instead of prosecuting them. Meanwhile, Buhari does nothing for the injured survivors of terrorism or the families of the dead.

Buhari's term ends in June next year, 2023. There are three significant contenders; one is another Fulani Muslim from the North, a kinsman of Buhari. Another is a Muslim from the South who has chosen a Muslim and allegedly Boko Haram sympathizer from the North as his vice president (called the Muslim-Muslim ticket), and the third is a Christian from the South. What is worrisome about the Muslim-Muslim ticket is that the presidential candidate is old, looks fragile, and allegedly sickly; if he wins and dies in office, then the vice president, another "Fulani kinsman," and Boko Haram strongman will take over. As a result, the Christian Association of Nigeria (CAN), the Christian umbrella association in Nigeria, have declared the only Christian running for president as their candidate.

Prayers and strategic meetings are being organized by Christians all over Nigeria for the coming election, one of them by the alumni of my university's Christian union. In the rendezvous, a well-established prophet said that the Lord told him, among other things, that the Muslim-Muslim ticket would win. I was taken aback by the responses of my well-educated, well-seasoned Christian to him. The vast majority were displeased, with some calling him names and accusing him of speaking by lying spirits. None of them bothered to pray on it or said that the Lord told them the prophecy was false; they just disliked it, then dismissed it and attacked the Prophet. Would these friends not join them to kill the prophets of God if they had come and were there in Israel during the Old Testament?

But they mocked the messengers of God, despised His words, and scoffed at His prophets, until the wrath of the Lord arose against His people, till there was no remedy (2chr. 36: 16, NKJV).

Today, prophets are the most persecuted ministry gift in the Church—from outright denial and repudiation of their ministries to ridiculing their personalities and ministries. Yes, we have a lot of false prophets but also false Teachers, Pastors, and Evangelists. We have a lot of fringe elements in the prophetic circles but so do all other ministry gifts. The devil uses both Believers and unbelievers to attack prophets and broadly uses the name to classify every false minister today.

Satan ridicules prophets because of their importance in the Body of Christ. The most significant problem on earth is blindness and confusion, mainly under the prophets' ministries to remove. Progress is not about speed but direction; if you are overspeeding in the wrong direction, you're not making progress but moving away from it. If you are in the right direction but traveling slowly, you are making progress. Confusion reigns where there is no prophet; that is the reason for the question in the Bible, "Is there no prophet here?"

As stated in the Preface, we have eloquent folks who hold down the truth in unrighteousness today and claim that there are no Apostles and Prophets. They truthfully have no single Scripture to back up their claim, as serious as it is, other than excesses of some fringe elements in the prophetic community.

An examination of the calling of many prophets in the Bible shows how difficult they were. Jeremiah, in the passage quoted above, seems to speak for them all—they were better off by politically correct and human standards than to heed the Lord's call and risk the people's anger. Still, when the Almighty puts a hook in your jaw, His call is no escaping. Thank God, the Lord is always with His servants.

I encourage every prophet and prophetic vessel to stand firm. If God has spoken through your mouth, the last laugh is yours. I also want to remove misgivings from the heart of genuine Christians. Even if you have been misinformed about Prophets and their prophetic gifts, you only need sincerity. Nobody kicks a dead dog, and the unbridled assault on the prophets is due to their importance in the Body of Christ.

Ignoring God's provisions and denying His ways is not intelligent, and those who want to recreate the Church of God in their own image are pumped up with self-righteousness. I have met people who pretend to be holier than God and like to amend His Words.

It is always a privilege to stand with God no matter how veracious our opponents are because:

There is no wisdom or understanding Or counsel against the Lord (Pro. 21: 30, NKJV

3

The Burden of the Lord

This time, there is another burden on the prophets from the Lord. This is because of the Lord's passion for His people, to rescue them or warn them about the impending judgment and consequences of their sins and errors. Everyone that has received intercession for others will be familiar with the pains of a burden from that Lord whereby you groan by the Spirit of the Lord to deliver His people. The burden of a prophet is more. It surpasses groaning and spills over to the Lord, asking them to take inconvenient prophetic actions that dramatize and cement His coming judgment if they refuse to repent.

The Lord's scepter is of righteousness; everything He does, love, mercy, kindness, goodness, salvation, judgment, and justice, must be righteous. His people must understand His purpose and blessings and deserve punishment if they disobey. They must understand the weight of sin and the depth of His love. They deserve all their sentence when they can make an intelligent decision to follow God or reject Him, to repent from their sin, or carry on with disobedience.

Regarding the burden of the Lord, no other prophet comes close to Ezekiel, Isaiah, Hosea, and Jeremiah; their callings were not easy. While Hosea was made to marry a prostitute that was unfaithful to him to illustrate God's frustration with Israel, Ezekiel had it worse.

> *"Then lie on your left side and put the sin of the people of Israel upon yourself. You are to bear their sin for the number of days you lie on your side. I have assigned you the same number of days as the years of their sin. So for 390 days you will bear the sin of the people of Israel.*

> *"After you have finished this, lie down again, this time on your right side, and bear the sin of the people of Judah. I have assigned you 40 days, a day for each year. Turn your face toward the siege of Jerusalem and with bared arm prophesy against her. I will tie you up with ropes so that you cannot turn from one side to the other until you have finished the days of your siege.*

> *"Take wheat and barley, beans and lentils, millet and spelt; put them in a storage jar and use them to make bread for yourself. You are to eat it during the 390 days you lie on your side. Weigh out twenty shekels*

of food to eat each day and eat it at set times. 11 Also measure out a sixth of a hin of water and drink it at set times. Eat the food as you would a loaf of barley bread; bake it in the sight of the people, using human excrement for fuel." The Lord said, "In this way the people of Israel will eat defiled food among the nations where I will drive them."

Then I said, "Not so, Sovereign Lord! I have never defiled myself. From my youth until now I have never eaten anything found dead or torn by wild animals. No impure meat has ever entered my mouth."

"Very well," he said, "I will let you bake your bread over cow dung instead of human excrement." (Ezek. 4: 4-15, NIV)

Imagine the burden Ezekiel had to carry to demonstrate his people's sin and its impending consequences if they refused to repent!

Now consider the Prophet Isaiah's burden of walking naked and barefoot for three years to dramatize the message of the Lord!

In the year that Tartan came to Ashdod, when Sargon the king of Assyria sent him, and he fought against Ashdod and took it, 2 at the same time the Lord spoke by Isaiah the son of Amoz, saying, "Go, and remove the sackcloth from your body, and take your sandals off your feet." And he did so, walking naked and barefoot.

Then the Lord said, "Just as My servant Isaiah has walked naked and barefoot three years for a sign and a wonder against Egypt and Ethiopia, 4 so shall the king of Assyria lead away the Egyptians as prisoners and the Ethiopians as captives, young and old, naked and barefoot, with their buttocks uncovered, to the shame of Egypt (Isa. 20: 1-4, NKJV).

Next, consider Jeremiah's very unpopular and annoying prophecy to kings of different nations. Imagine if someone did that today—send yokes as prophetic souvenirs to presidents at the the General Debate of the United Nations General Assembly meeting with a message of doom and an impending loss of sovereignty!

"Thus says the Lord to me: 'Make for yourselves bonds and yokes, and put them on your neck, 3 and send them to the king of Edom, the king of Moab, the king of the Ammonites, the king of Tyre, and the king of Sidon, by the hand of the messengers who come to Jerusalem to Zedekiah king of Judah. 4 And command them to say to their masters, "Thus says the Lord of hosts, the God of Israel—thus you shall say to your masters: 5 'I have made the earth, the man and the beast that are on the ground, by My great power and by My outstretched arm, and have given it to whom it seemed proper to Me. 6 And now I have given all these lands into the hand of Nebuchadnezzar the king of Babylon, My servant; and the beasts of the field I have also given him to serve him. 7 So all nations shall serve him and his son

and his son's son, until the time of his land comes; and then many nations and great kings shall make him serve them. 8 And it shall be, that the nation and kingdom which will not serve Nebuchadnezzar the king of Babylon, and which will not put its neck under the yoke of the king of Babylon, that nation I will punish,' says the Lord, 'with the sword, the famine, and the pestilence, until I have consumed them by his hand (Jer. 27: 2-8, NKJV).

Prophets face opposition from fake prophets, political figures, their followers, Pastors, cessationists, and the ignorant and gullible.

Now the word of the Lord came to Jeremiah, after Hananiah the prophet had broken the yoke from the neck of the prophet Jeremiah, saying, 13 "Go and tell Hananiah, saying, 'Thus says the Lord: "You have broken the yokes of wood, but you have made in their place yokes of iron." 14 For thus says the Lord of hosts, the God of Israel: "I have put a yoke of iron on the neck of all these nations, that they may serve Nebuchadnezzar king of Babylon; and they shall serve him. I have given him the beasts of the field also." ' "

Then the prophet Jeremiah said to Hananiah the prophet, "Hear now, Hananiah, the Lord has not sent you, but you make this people trust in a lie. 16 Therefore thus says the Lord: 'Behold, I will cast you from the face of the earth. This year you shall die, because you have taught rebellion against the Lord.' "

So Hananiah the prophet died the same year in the seventh month (Jer. 28: 12-17, NKJV).

I have gone to this length to prove a point: it is not easy to be a prophet; it is not a calling for the lily-livered. You must obey the Lord and stand for Him against the people's popular opinion, with varying consequences. If you fear the people and don't deliver the message or water it down, you will run into the Lord's trouble. For the Prophet, it's often a case of "damn if you do, damn if you don't," however, it is wise to please the Lord and let the people please themselves.

When I say to the wicked, 'You shall surely die,' and you give him no warning, nor speak to warn the wicked from his wicked way, to save his life, that same wicked man shall die in his iniquity; but his blood I will require at your hand. 19 Yet, if you warn the wicked, and he does not turn from his wickedness, nor from his wicked way, he shall die in his iniquity; but you have delivered your soul.

"Again, when a righteous man turns from his righteousness and commits iniquity, and I lay a stumbling block before him, he shall die; because you did not give him warning, he shall die in his sin, and his righteousness which he has done shall not be remembered; but his blood I will require at your hand. 21 Nevertheless if you warn the righteous man that the righteous should not sin, and he does not sin, he shall surely live because he took warning; also you will have delivered your soul." (Ezek. 3: 18-21, NKJV).

Unlike the Evangelist, who is sent to unbelievers, the Prophet's primary calling is to Believers. They are ten times more difficult to minister to when they slip into unbelief and rebellion. Many prophets were brutally murdered, like Isaiah, Ezekiel, and Jeremiah, because they spoke for God!

And He said to me: "Son of man, I am sending you to the children of Israel, to a rebellious nation that has rebelled against Me; they and their fathers have transgressed against Me to this very day. For they are impudent and stubborn children. I am sending you to them, and you shall say to them, 'Thus says the Lord God. As for them, whether they hear or whether they refuse—for they are a rebellious house—yet they will know that a prophet has been among them.

"And you, son of man, do not be afraid of them nor be afraid of their words, though briers and thorns are with you and you dwell among scorpions; do not be afraid of their words or dismayed by their looks, though they are a rebellious house. 7 You shall speak My words to them, whether they hear or whether they refuse, for they are rebellious (Ezek. 2: 3-6, NKJV).

But the house of Israel will not listen to you, because they will not listen to Me; for all the house of Israel are impudent and hard-hearted. 8 Behold, I have made your face strong against their faces, and your forehead strong against their foreheads. 9 Like adamant stone, harder than flint, I have made your forehead; do not be afraid of them, nor be dismayed

*at their looks, though they are a rebellious house."
(Ezek. 3: 7-9, NKJV).*

*Then I heard the voice of the Lord saying, "Whom
shall I send? And who will go for us?" And I said,
"Here am I. Send me!" He said, "Go and tell this
people:*

*"'Be ever hearing, but never understanding; be ever
seeing, but never perceiving.' Make the heart of this
people calloused; make their ears dull and close their
eyes. Otherwise, they might see with their eyes, hear
with their ears, understand with their hearts, and
turn and be healed." Then I said, "For how long,
Lord?" And he answered: "Until the cities lie ruined
and without inhabitant, until the houses are left
deserted, and the fields ruined and ravaged, until
the Lord has sent everyone far away and the land is
utterly forsaken. And though a tenth remains in the
land, it will again be laid waste. But as the terebinth
and oak leave stumps when they are cut down, so the
holy seed will be the stump in the land." (Isa. 6: 8-13,
NIV).*

Every true prophet deserves prayers, love, and respect
because their calling makes them prone to attacks,
confrontation, and hatred.

The Lord does not want to use us but longs to work in
partnership with us. He desires fellowship and wants
to reveal His ways to us. Our distance from Him
reduces us to tools instead of partners. World

evangelization shall be done without tears; by God's partners.

And they went out and preached everywhere, the Lord working with them and confirming the word through the accompanying signs. Amen (Mark 16: 20, NKJV)

4

Prophets & Their Ministries

The ministries of prophets are the most regulated in the Holy Bible. This removes any justification from any Church or denomination to be afraid of prophets or reject their ministries. Human beings have a penchant for making their own rules—a sign of power, domination, and stupidity. For example, churches will not invite any minister outside their denomination or movement under the guise of protecting their flock from false doctrines. What do they do to their pastors who preach heresies?

If that is their genuine concern, why don't they give the invited ministers from outside their movement a list of what they believe and make them agree not to teach something different before they come? Why don't they inform the guest minister that they are duty-bound to correct any other thing they said right to their face after the message? If the discrepancy is too much, is it wrong if they stop the message? Would anyone blame them for that? Don't they know that the Body of Christ is far more extensive than any denomination and has more gifts, by far, than theirs? When a simple thing becomes rocket science to intelligent people, you know they are playing games. If we find reasons to impeach God's words and provisions, like denying Spiritual gifts and the ministries of the Apostles and Prophets, we are editing God's words and questioning His wisdom, which comes at a very high cost.

The Ten Fingers of a Prophet's Ministry

a) The prophetic ministry has gained momentum in the Evangelical and Pentecostal circles after a long and regrettable absence—both for right and wrong reasons. The misgivings, however, are not reducing, no thanks to some Prophets who are less prophetic in their conducts, operations, and ministerial etiquette than is written in the Holy Scriptures. Pastors often have problems with folks with simple gifts of prophecy, let alone prophets. It is the same abuse knocking hard on the so-called "Apostolic movement," whereby some self-appointed Apostles try to lord it over pastors, exercising power where they had none or had sown. The reactions are similar in some quarters—outright denial of Apostolic and Prophetic ministries, thereby adding fire to the Ceasationists, the modern-day Sadducees. They make themselves known by what they oppose rather than what they stand for.

b) Thankfully, the Holy Bible is clear on the ministries of the Prophet; and perhaps is harder on it than any other ministry in the so-named "Five-fold Ministries." There are no excesses left unaddressed in the scriptures among prophets. However, Pastors, Teachers, and Evangelists have their problems too. For example, the rampart disunity in the Body of Christ today—our worst weakness of all times—is traceable primarily to Teachers and pastors who are so territorial that they build doctrines and ministries around their own personality, prejudice, limitations, traditions, etc.

c) As a guide to the body of Christ on the ministry of prophets, I have identified ten cardinal points to know about Prophets and their ministries. Five of these are for every Believer to understand the ministries of Prophets, while the remaining five dwell on biblical controls and balances of the ministries of Prophets. Therefore, I would like to call each group of five "The Five Fingers of the Prophetic Hand." This is for the church and secondarily for the Prophets.

d) The five fingers for the Church.

Finger 1:   There are different kinds of prophets:

Since a Prophet is an Oracle of God or God's mouthpiece, we need to know at what level of grace they operate and the attendant limitations and authority. Three groups of prophets are seen in the

Bible: Seers, Prophets, and False Prophets. In practice today, we also noticed a group I call "Interpreters"— and I mean no insult. These prophets specialize mainly in decoding Old Testament types, shadows, and practices while drawing parallels in the New Testament, interpreting natural and political events, and predicting the future. They tend to bring out revelations and prophecies in everything, which sometimes may not have practical applications. However, the Holy Bible is prominent that prophecy does not come from human knowledge or will. I often said that "Word of knowledge" is different from "Word from knowledge":

> *for prophecy never came by the will of man, but holy men of God spoke as they were moved by the Holy Spirit (2Pet. 1:21, NKJV)*

A broken clock is right twice a day; while these permutations could be right sometimes, it is fair to say that they are not prophecies. For our purpose, I'll limit myself mainly to the first two while observing the remaining groups.

THE SEER

There are two Hebrew words translated as a seer in the Bible: raah (to see vision) and choseh (a beholder of vision). However, one word consistently translated as Prophet; is the Hebrew word "Navi" meaning "An inspired man." The question is, "How does a Seer differ from a Prophet, or are these different names for the same person?" What we observed in the Scriptures is that some people are consistently called Seers while others are consistently called Prophets, e.g., 1Chr. 29:29 says Samuel the Seer, Nathan the Prophet, Gad the Seer; 2 Chr. 9:29 says Nathan Prophet, Iddo Seer; 2Chr. 12:15 says Shemaiah Prophet, Iddo Seer; 2Chr. 29:25 says Gad Seer, Nathan Prophet, etc. So, Nathan was always Prophet, while Gad and Iddo were consistently Seers. Only Samuel was called both a Seer and Prophet (1Chr. 29:29; 1 Sam. 3:20; 19:20), while Gad was called God's Prophet, David's Seer (2 Sam. 24: 11). Another observation is that the Bible did mention "All the Prophets and all the Seers" (2 Kings 17: 13; Isa. 29: 10) clearly showing them as distinct. Now kindly keep a lid on their differences meanwhile.

THE PROPHET

As stated above, the word translated as "Prophet" means "An inspired one." However, of great insight is 1 Sam. 9:9(NIV):

(Formerly in Israel, if someone went to inquire of God, they would say, "Come, let us go to the seer," because the prophet of today used to be called a seer.)

When you consider the above passage in light of the observations above, it is clear that the ministry of a Seer progressed into a Prophet as grace increased with responsibility in the land of Israel. It is noteworthy that the Prophet's ministry only gained currency in stormy times of misrule and ungodliness. For example, Elijah wouldn't have gotten such an eventful ministry had he come during the time of a righteous king like David. He wouldn't encounter the prophets of Baal, wouldn't have to stop the rain, and wouldn't run from the Queen (Jezebel). Further, the angel, widow, and ravens will not have to feed him, nor will he have to appear or disappear. So, as the nation of Israel drifts away from God, the responsibility of Seers increased from just revealing secrets to discerning the mind of God by pointing the nation in the right direction.

Simply put, a Prophet is a teaching Seer. A prophet or an inspired man can "see" and "teach." In the book of Isaiah, chapter 30, verse 10, we see that a Seer sees while a Prophet prophesies. Daniel was a Seer since he saw visions but taught no one. We also noticed that Daniel's visions required him to pray for explanations; however, we see prophets see visions while at the same time being inspired to add, "Thus says the Lord...." However, the veracity and accuracy of Daniel's visions of the End-Time prove that a Seer is not necessarily inferior to a Prophet, only that a prophet does more.

Now Samuel was called both Seer and Prophet. However, examinations of his ministry reveal that he was more of a seer than a Prophet, considering the scarcity of the word of God in his time (1 Sam. 3: 1). The word of God must not be scarce in the ministry of a prophet.

These tell us that a Seer's ministration is hardly "wholistic." Perhaps you have met people who can tell you your problems and phone numbers and got you knocked down to the floor under the power, but your yoke remains unbroken. Or even when the yoke is broken, you still don't find direction to the mountain top.

Most of the problems associated with the prophetic ministry today are caused by Seers who are gifted but not sound in the word of God. Every Seer must remember Balaam, a Prophet or Seer turned Sorcerer (Jos. 13: 22; 2 Pet. 2: 16). It is always problematic to build a ministry around the gifts of the Holy Spirit. Each gospel minister owes it to God to study His word into His approval so that they can correctly explain the word of God (2 Tim. 2: 15).

Finger 2:   Prophetic ministry has dual purpose:

Prophetic grace is one thing that must be tied to its purpose; otherwise, the abuse attendant could be of immense proportion. A cursory look into the Bible clearly shows the dual purpose of the Prophets' ministries: divine help and judgment.

Divine Help

At that time the prophets Haggai and Zechariah son of Iddo prophesied to the Jews in Judah and Jerusalem. They prophesied in the name of the God of Israel who was over them. 2 Zerubbabel son of Shealtiel and Jeshua son of Jehozadak responded by starting again to rebuild the Temple of God in Jerusalem. And the prophets of God were with them and helped them. (Ezra 5: 1-2, NLB)

There is a divine enterprise on the planet earth, and the most critical purpose of the prophetic ministry is to help every hand in God's vineyard to establish it by dint of prophetic grace. Wherever there is a prophet and respect for the prophetic grace, God's enterprise fortifies.

And by a prophet the LORD brought Israel out of Egypt, and by a prophet was he preserved. (Hosea 12: 13, KJV)

But he that prophesies speaks unto men to edification, and exhortation, and comfort. (1 Cor. 14: 3, KJ2000)

Hosea gave us a panoramic view of the prophetic help—to bring people out of trouble and preserve them from corruption. Brother Paul gave us the "EEC" of prophecy: edification, exhortation, and comfort.

Prophetic help comes in two ways: it connects you with grace and mercy and points you in the right direction. At times, all you need is either direction or backup by the power of God. However, it is incomplete if you need all, and a prophetic ministration doesn't achieve them. A prophet or prophetic vessel must always trust God for complete prophetic assistance—to point people in the divine direction and back them up with mercy, power, and grace.

I was a guest minister in a church in North America

when I gave a man word from the Lord. He was involved in a kind of fraud that could send him to jail for many years, was put on bail, and was about to face trial when I came to his church. He was panicky and depressed, but I told him not to worry because "I saw that the case has been withdrawn in the Spirit realm." He believed and brightened up. He went to trial, but the case was dropped, and he returned home a free man. This man received prophetic direction as well as divine backing and grace.

Meanwhile, about seventeen years ago, I was ministering in a church in the EU when I called out a woman and gave her a word from the Lord, "You are full of activities in this church. You run around to make things happen in this church and put down big money financing this church; however, the Lord asks me to tell you that you are living in sin. He says that you cannot bribe Him and that if you really want to serve Him, you need to repent from your sins and that He will deposit greet gifts in you to make you serve Him greatly...." This woman went on the floor under the anointing of the Holy Spirit. Her Pastor confirmed every word given to her.

This lady only needed direction as salvation from sin is only got through faith in Jesus Christ alone. However, when I met her two years later in another church, she told me that she was no longer a worker in the church because she realized the futility of serving God while living in sin. I asked her the problem, and she confessed that she was hooked on adultery because her husband was bedridden and living in another country. She wouldn't accept that she could do without it with the help of God. This woman found prophetic direction but wouldn't cooperate with God to find deliverance! This was a complete but unsuccessful ministration from a Prophet's point of view.

A perfect example of a complete prophetic ministration in the Scriptures is what is recorded of Elisha in 2 Kings 3 (note verses 16-18):

> *And he said, "Thus says the LORD: 'Make this valley full of ditches.' For thus says the LORD: 'You shall not see wind, nor shall you see rain; yet that valley shall be filled with water, so that you, your cattle, and your animals may drink.' And this is a simple matter in the sight of the LORD; He will also deliver the Moabites into your hand. Also you shall attack every fortified city and every choice city, and shall cut down every good tree, and stop up every spring of water, and ruin every good piece of land with stones." Now it happened in the morning, when the grain offering was offered, that suddenly water came by way of Edom, and the land was filled with water.*

The rest of the chapter described how the word of the Prophet came to pass, and the three stranded kings found direction and divine backing!

Divine Judgment

We see Prophets foretelling or pronouncing divine judgments on nations and individuals throughout the

Old Testament. This was a rarity in the New Testament mainly because we are in the time of grace and the focus is to proclaim the Good News of God's sovereign pardon for mankind everywhere through Christ. Nevertheless, we see Paul pronouncing divine judgment on Elymas (Acts 13: 8-12) and how Peter stood in divine judgment against Ananias and Sapphira (Acts 5: 1-10).

Yes, I know that Paul and Peter were Apostles, but an Apostle is basically someone who can function in all the ministry-gift offices. Paul was a Prophet and Teacher before becoming an Apostle (Acts 13: 1).

Around 2000, I was watching television in Lagos, Nigeria, when a "White garment" false prophet with dreadlocks came on, prophesying blasphemy on that nation. As I watched, I got furious—and anger induced by the Holy Spirit, and I pointed the finger at the TV set and pronounced, "You will not prophesy again! You just prophesied your very last lies." About two months later, he died!

I was also in North America ministering when I called out a couple and gave them an open warning to prepare for a devastating visitation from the Lord, except they changed their divisive activity in the church. I later found out that they had grievances and misgivings against their pastor, which was getting in the way of the Lord. Members were leaving the church rapidly, and gossip was driving the grapevine in the city. Thankfully, I could mediate and secure a soft landing for these folks.

I have a few other examples on this point that I am unwilling to share currently because of their sensitivity. It is, however, sufficient to say that divine judgment is the unusual purpose of the prophetic ministry in the New Testament Church. We must also remember that God is not happy to see a sinner die, and we shouldn't be in a hurry but be willing to wait for judgment day. However, often, someone sadly needs to be a scapegoat, and that also falls under the ministry of a prophet.

Finger 3: God owns the message; the prophet owns delivery:

There are four parts to a prophecy:

1. What God actually said, showed, or impressed, etc.,

2. How the Prophet understood it in light of the Word of God

3. How the Prophet delivers the message

4. The Prophet's recommendations on the prophecy.

Often, church folks fail to realize that there may be a gap between what God said and how the Prophet understood and delivered it. Many times, message delivery is the reason why the Prophet is rejected. It is, as a matter of fact, in the delivery that the message can get corrupted because it is where the Prophet's own humanity, temperament, prejudice, misgivings, gaffes, anger, etc., get in the way of the message.

For example, if Nathan were John the Baptist, how do you think he would confront David on the issue of his adultery and murder? God told Samuel to anoint David during a sacrifice smokescreen, clearly informing us that message delivery requires wisdom and tact. It is indiscretion to spit fire when you don't have the anointing to bring the rain, as you simply could be consumed in the inferno you created.

However, no matter the delivery faults, the prophetic word remains God's intention; therefore, it is dangerous to reject prophecy because of its mode of delivery, which may be caustic or unwise. This is what I mean: a prophet was attending a wedding solemnization in the church in West Africa when he prophesied, "Joshua (not real name), take no other wife after this one, Joshua, take no other wife after this one...." Of course, he was severely rebuked by all and sundry—ostracized and rejected.

The Prophet's mode of delivery lacked wisdom, no doubt, but the baby was thrown out with the birth water. The message was stopped midway and rejected altogether. However, a few years later, that wife died, and everybody realized too late that the Prophet spoke by the Spirit of God. Things could have been different if the kernel of the message had been taken and prayed against.

It is common today to hear a prophet give a powerful

prophecy by the Spirit of God only to go ahead and spoil it by recommending funny things to be done. This is common with prophets who are shallow in the word of God; therefore, he brings his native myths, taboo, innuendos, ignorance, etc., into the message, thereby turning a good word from the Lord into a concoction to be separated and discerned.

Finger 4:   Prophetic Ifs Abound:

God, by nature, does not give freedom or blessings without responsibilities, unlike governments in the Western world. Again, everything God created is good; therefore, man is good enough to do what God created him to do. Yes, we need divine intervention, but God will not take over duties assigned to us; He has elected to do things with us and through us on earth. In Psalm 15: 16, we read:

> *The heaven, even the heavens, are the LORD's; But the earth He has given to the children of men. (NKJV)*

The earth is given! Did you get that? Perhaps you've listened to powerful ministers who said that Adam committed treason and transferred ownership of the earth to Satan at the fall of man. They also back their claim up with what Satan told Jesus Christ while tempting him that the world's kingdoms have been given to him. Well, this teaching is nothing but extra-Biblical; and lacks commonsense. Satan's brand is disobedience to God, and his language is lies; he is not worthy of trust, and you're stupid to believe him.

It is a fact that the Holy Bible never refers to Adam as the god of the earth. When God puts him in the Garden of Eden, didn't He give him instructions on what to eat, not eat, and to tend the Garden? God is the Landlord of the earth! He judges nations when they rebel and once wipes out life on earth while saving some. Adam had no "title deed" to this planet to transfer, as widely taught. Satan is "the god of the world" (2Cor. 4), referring to the world system, not the earth as a real estate.

What happened to Adam was simple; he disobeyed God and was alienated from Him, exposing and making him vulnerable to the devil. God has never given away His sovereignty over the earth, and David said above that this planet still belongs to mankind even long after Adam's fall.

You, therefore, have a role to play in bringing personal prophesies given to you to pass in your life. That is why personal prophecies, just like God's promises, are not done deals in themselves but are subject to conditions. I will give four examples from the Bible:

Josiah died contrary to the personal prophecy given to him:

> *But as for the king of Judah, who sent you to inquire of the LORD, in this manner you shall speak to him, 'Thus says the LORD God of Israel... "Surely,*

therefore, I will gather you to your fathers, and you shall be gathered to your grave in peace; and your eyes shall not see all the calamity which I will bring on this place.""" So they brought back word to the king (2 Kings 22: 18-20, NKJV).

It is noteworthy, however, that Josiah did not die in peace as promised by God, and God is not to blame:

... Necho king of Egypt came up to fight against Carchemish by the Euphrates; and Josiah went out against him. But he sent messengers to him, saying, "What have I to do with you, king of Judah? I have not come against you this day, but against the house with which I have war; for God commanded me to make haste. Refrain from meddling with God, who is with me, lest He destroy you." Nevertheless Josiah would not turn his face from him, but disguised himself so that he might fight with him, and did not heed the words of Necho from the mouth of God. So he came to fight in the Valley of Megiddo. 23 And the archers shot King Josiah; and the king said to his servants, "Take me away, for I am severely wounded." 24 His servants therefore took him out of that chariot and put him in the second chariot that he had, and they brought him to Jerusalem. So he died, and was buried in one of the tombs of his fathers. And all Judah and Jerusalem mourned for Josiah (2 Chr. 35: 20-24, NKJV).

So, why did Josiah die contrary to Prophetess Huldah's word from the Lord? Firstly, he went to war without clearance from the Lord. Secondly, he probably disdained Pharaoh Necho's claim that God sent him on an errand because Necho was an unbeliever; he failed to realize that God is sovereign and reserves the right to use anyone and anything He created. Thirdly, Josiah probably became self-conceited in the face of his obedience to God and his significant reforms. He, therefore, stepped outside of God's will.

Ephraim, a perfect example of a lifestyle unworthy of prophetic blessing:

Perhaps you remember how Jacob put the blessing of the right hand on Ephraim and proclaimed that he would be greater than his elder brother, Manasseh (Gen. 48: 1-20). Ephraim, however, did not stay with the Lord and, as a tribe, joined himself to idols, thereby losing superiority (Hosea 4: 17; 5: 11; 7: 8-10). Manasseh became more substantial to the point that when twelve thousand would be saved from each tribe of Israel in the coming tribulation, Manasseh replaced Ephraim! (Rev. 7: 6).

Israel's extra 30 years in slavery:

> *Then He said to Abram: "Know certainly that your descendants will be strangers in a land that is not theirs, and will serve them, and they will afflict them four hundred years. And also the nation whom they serve I will judge; afterward they shall come out with great possessions (Gen. 15: 13-14, NKJV).*

> *Now the sojourn of the children of Israel who lived in*

Egypt was four hundred and thirty years (Exo. 12: 40, NKJV).

Here we see the Almighty God, all-seeing and all-knowing, said to Abraham that his descendants would spend 400 years in slavery; however, by the time Israel left Egypt, they had spent 30 years extra. This shows the difference between God's intention and man's compliance. Moses, the man God was grooming to lead Israel out of Egypt, moved prematurely and ten years too early and finally went on self-exile. Forty years later, when God finally sorted him out, Israel had languished in slavery past the prophetic time. God's usual choice is to work through the system, making our choices very important to our spiritual and physical welfare.

Zechariah's prophecy on Christ:

"Rejoice greatly, O daughter of Zion! Shout, O daughter of Jerusalem! Behold, your King is coming to you; He is just and having salvation, Lowly and riding on a donkey, A colt, the foal of a donkey (Zech. 9: 9).

Now when they drew near Jerusalem, and came to Bethphage, at the Mount of Olives, then Jesus sent two disciples, saying to them, "Go into the village opposite you, and immediately you will find a donkey tied, and a colt with her. Loose them and bring them to Me. And if anyone says anything to you, you shall say, 'The Lord has need of them,' and immediately he will send them." All this was done that it might be fulfilled which was spoken by the prophet, saying: " Tell the daughter of Zion, ' Behold, your King is coming to you, Lowly, and sitting on a donkey, A colt, the foal of a donkey.'" (Matt. 21: 1-5)

When the time came for Christ to ride a donkey to Jerusalem, Zechariah's prophecy was threatened! No one gave Him the donkey, and only one village separated Him from Jerusalem. The Lord would have walked where prophecy said He would ride. Verse 4 of Matthew chapter 25 is vital to everyone who cares to study the subject of prophecy:

"All this was done that it might be fulfilled, which was spoken by the prophet, saying...."

Now, if Christ had to do something to bring a prophecy to pass on His life, how about you? King David put it this way:

27 For You, O LORD of hosts, God of Israel, have revealed this to Your servant, saying, 'I will build you a house.' Therefore Your servant has found it in his heart to pray this prayer to You (2 Sam. 7: 27).

Finger 5: The Prophet's ministry in the Old Testament is different from the New Testament:

" And it shall come to pass afterward That I will pour out My Spirit on all flesh; Your sons and your

daughters shall prophesy, Your old men shall dream dreams, Your young men shall see visions. And also on My menservants and on My maidservants I will pour out My Spirit in those days (Joel 2: 28-29).

Fulfillment of Joel's prophecy must have profound implications both for the Prophet and the Body of Christ at large—and it did right from day one when it came to pass on the day of Pentecost:

a) Hearing or knowing God's voice was declassified as His Spirit is poured out on ALL flesh and no longer the exclusive reserve of some people. Also, notice that two categories of the gifts of the Holy Spirit were mentioned to go with the Spirit's outpouring: Prophecy (an inspiration gift); dreams and visions (revelation gifts). Joel said these gifts would be signs of the Holy Spirit's outpour on all flesh. It means, therefore, that Believers would not walk in darkness. It, therefore, means that though we can't all be prophets, we can and should all be prophetic.

b) In the Old Testament, a prophet is judged when his prophecy comes to pass or fails to come to pass; however, in the New Testament, there is an instant check on their originality since the same Spirit dwells in all Believers (Deut. 18: 22; 1 Cor. 14: 29). A prophet, therefore, shouldn't give prophecies in manners that would prevent others to judge the prophecy; for example, no prophet should give prophetic word privately to a church member without the knowledge of the Pastor or the elders. Again, it is unconscionable to arrange private meetings, either at home or elsewhere, beyond the reach or permission of the Pastor. Prophecies given under that circumstance could be unchecked and unexamined. This kind of action often divides the church, afford the prophet to carry away disciples after himself and thereby go into errors and unexamined prophecies.

c) With some exceptions of revelation prophecies, prophecies are usually given to confirm what God has been saying to you. In cases where it is not a confirmation, you must watch it prayerfully.

However, a New Testament prophet should have a tougher skin because prophecies are often hurriedly and wrongly judged by Pastors, Elders, and individuals depending on their depth in the word of God and spiritual discernment. I have given prophecies that were instantly rejected in the past, only for the prophecies to pass as given. A good example is a prophecy I gave a bosom friend several years ago that the Lord calls him into a full-time ministry. He rejected it instantly, saying that I prophesied from my mind. However, this fellow is a full-time resident pastor of a thriving church today.

More often than not, my prophecies are rejected for "being too accurate"; I've heard it said that somebody must have leaked secrets to me to be that accurate!

Meanwhile, it is difficult to judge some prophecies. The more accessible part is that no true prophecy can contradict the written Word of God. After a prophecy passes that test comes discernment by the Spirit of God, and this is where most people fail while judging prophecies. For example, I had a friend who married a beautiful singer in their denomination's Choir that turned out to be heavily possessed of demons. They ran into terrible problems, including sicknesses and demonic harassment. Then a Pastor fasted for three days praying for them. He came up with what the Lord told him: this woman must be prayed for beside a named river to cast out the demons from her, and she must not come home with the dress she wore to the riverside.

Everybody was angry with him because he talked like a witch doctor—there is no way you ask Evangelicals to do that because it looks fetish. The husband was particularly incensed with the Pastor. In the process, the husband temporarily backslid under the yoke of his wife's witchcraft and took her to a witch doctor. The witch doctor confronted her on her willful covenant with the goddess of the river that the Pastor mentioned earlier. His wife collapsed and died. It was then that everybody believed that the Pastor truly heard from the Lord. Since the Holy Bible says that the things of the Spirit are spiritually discerned, judging a prophecy sometimes requires the ability to hear from God.

5

Prophets & Their Seatbelt

This chapter will look at the Five Fingers of the Prophetic Hand—For the Prophet. The prophetic anointing could be intoxicating, while the ministry could be very influential. However, the ministries of the Prophets are not without brakes and seatbelts. In fact, Scripture says that "The spirits of the Prophets are subject to the Prophets" (1Cor. 14: 32). Therefore, there is a need for the prophet to hold himself close to avoid a descent into errors, manipulations, control attitude, etc., that are common with some prophetic ministries. In this discourse, I will zero in on issues peculiar to the prophetic ministry:

Finger 1: A prophet MUST be versatile in the word of God

It is ridiculous to prophesy the word of God without in-depth knowledge of His written word! The word of God is the language of God; to speak for Him without being fluent in His language is obviously prone to errors. While a prophet may not be a teacher (as in the case of Seers), he must be sound in God's word. Experienced pastors know how to groom members to balance their lever of gifts and knowledge of the word of God. The following is my advice for everyone in the prophetic ministry:

The word of God is light (Pro. 6: 23); therefore, to walk outside his word is to walk in darkness, which makes one prone to falling into ditches, traps, and injuries. Everything a prophet does must be scriptural. In fact, the Bible says to prophesy in proportion to faith (Rom. 12: 6), and I know what that means. I have prophesied in Ireland and the US on three different ladies at different times, each of them a single mother of 2, that they will get married; two of them within the year, and in fact, one of the prophecies came in July, and none was engaged at the time.

All of them got married precisely as spoken by the Lord. However, several years ago, I gave the word to a single lady in her forties: she would get married to someone coming from a faraway country. But then I couldn't sleep after that because she gave me £100 in an envelope with a note, "I am donating this money believing that your prophecy will come to pass." It was Nottingham, and the prophecy came to pass the following year when a man came from the USA to marry her.

In fact, the highest level of prophecy is revelatory teaching that point people in God's direction. In this situation, a prophet's teaching becomes the x-ray of the present or the future events of the people's lives, such that they receive grace and power to stand in God's purpose and victory. We see flashes of this under every Ministry Gift, but this is the terrain of prophets.

A Seer is a budding prophet and, therefore, must develop himself in the word of God. It is better to put himself under the tutelage of a prophet as it is dangerous to build a ministry around the gifts.

A prophet must draw the line between doctrines and his prophetic gifting. This is necessary to prevent doctrines based on experience but not the word of God. Christ spat on the ground and anointed a blind man with the clay; if this happened at the hands of some Prophets, they could build a doctrine like "The spiritual mystery of clay!" Of course, Adam was formed with clay!! I've seen that doctrines are built on prophetic experiences leading to severe errors. Every prophet must make an effort not to descend into superstitious doctrines because people will swallow anything so long the anointing is flowing and testimonies are pouring out. We must all remember that Samson threw away the donkey's jawbone!

When he came to Lehi, the Philistines came shouting against him. Then the Spirit of the Lord came mightily upon him; and the ropes that were on his arms became like flax that is burned with fire, and his bonds broke loose from his hands. He found a fresh jawbone of a donkey, reached out his hand and took it, and killed a thousand men with it. Then Samson said:

"With the jawbone of a donkey, Heaps upon heaps, With the jawbone of a donkey I have slain a thousand men!"

And so it was, when he had finished speaking, that he threw the jawbone from his hand, and called that place Ramath Lehi (Jud. 15: 14-17, NKJV).

Today, the jawbone will become something else! It would be touted as a contact point, and replicas could be made to tap the anointing at a fee!!

One sensitive area to watch is what a prophet prescribes after delivering his message; in Africa, well-gifted prophets make unscriptural recommendations based on the practices of their denomination. For example, there is a particular denomination that believes in praying. They are fond of recommending psalms to be read on the water in the wee hours of the night, both for drinking and bathing. These are not false prophets, but their denomination started long ago in the formative years of Christianity in West Africa when the knowledge of the word was scarce in the face of solid occultism and black magic. However, the practice remains. However, if they wish to minister to the larger body of Christ, particularly the Evangelical, Pentecostal, and Charismatic stork, they must adhere strictly to the word of God. Traditions must give way to the word of God.

Finger 2: A Prophet must beware of simony

Simony is the selling or buying of ecclesiastical or spiritual privileges; therefore, it is simoniacal for a prophet to extort money by using his gifting. In African circles today, prophetic ministrations are closely associated with fundraising. Some prophets only minister to raise money; I have seen prophets asking people to give money so God can help them out of their troubles. Some of them are even bold enough to say something like, "If you can give me" this or that amount, then meet me tomorrow for special prayers!

A prophet must trust God for his needs and not be tempted to put his gifting for sale. Nehemiah described Shemaiah as a hireling of Tobiah and Sanballat against him (Neh. 6: 10-12). How many prophets are hirelings today? We have cases whereby a Pastor invites you to minister in his church for a deal—fifty percent of all money raised belongs to you while fifty percent belongs to him. Balaam loves money and, as a result, went from being a prophet to a Soothsayer, as explained above. To every simoniac, remember Gehazi (2 Kings 5: 20-27); a prophet who craves money is only a step away from becoming a false prophet. In fact, one trademark of false prophets is their love of money.

Having said that, let me balance this fact: Priests in the Bible were remunerated with the people's tithe. However, prophets are not so reimbursed. It was standard practice in Israel not to go to a prophet empty-handed, as demonstrated in 1 Sam. 9: 6-8. Well, prophets are God's conduit pipe of blessings; now, the blessing is the opposite of a curse. If a curse without reason will not land, then an unprovoked blessing may not land! When we talk of grace in the Body of Christ, kindly understand that it is only free for us; for our Lord Jesus Christ, who made it possible, it is the costliest thing ever! That was why Isaac asked Esau to go hunt some wild game and prepare it to taste "that my soul may bless you" (Gen. 27: 4). When you sow into prophetic grace, it robs off on you. However, this truth shouldn't be exploited or twisted to practice greed; simony will ultimately be judged by our God.

Finger 3: It could be suicidal for a prophet to lack wisdom.

A prophet without wisdom must be pitied indeed. You need the wisdom to manage yourself, the people, and even the prophetic anointing. A prophet must not forget that if you deliver a message that God has not sent you, then you are on your own. Indeed, there is a difference between the "word of knowledge" and the "word from knowledge!" Often, prophets are pushed to prophesy or speak to people from knowledge, resulting in catastrophic results. John the Baptist is a good example here.

Even when the prophecy comes from God, a prophet requires skill to deliver it. Kudos here go to Nathan and Samuel, wise prophets. When Samuel complained to God that Saul would kill him if he anointed David king, God taught him wisdom on how to do it. God could have decided to back him up with power, but He chose wisdom. Yes, when Saul wanted to kill David in the bosom of Samuel, the Lord defended him with His power (1 Sam. 19: 20-24).

A prophet also cannot operate everywhere; something about that anointing wouldn't flow in the presence of sin except to deliver judgment. In 2 Kings 3: 13-15, we see how the presence of King Joram, Ahab's son, affected Elisha such that he had to request a Minstrel before anointing came on him. Not a few times have I found myself in such tense positions that I know God is not with the people. However, wisdom from that passage above is that a prophet must not joke with music; actually, any prophet who can afford it should have his own minstrels, which isn't a luxury. Whenever anointing is lifting in a prophetic ministration, good music can bring it back.

One all-important point I want to point out to prophets today is written in 1 Sam. 10: 5 (NIV):

> *"After that you will go to Gibeah of God, where there is a Philistine outpost. As you approach the town, you will meet a procession of prophets coming down from the high place with lyres, timbrels, pipes and harps being played before them, and they will be prophesying.*

Prophets in the Bible banded together; the above passage reveals a practice that we need today! Here we saw a procession of prophets, and wherever two or three prophets were gathered, there was music!! And there are prophecies!!! In Acts 13: 1-2, we also read:

> *Now in the church at Antioch there were prophets and teachers: Barnabas, Simeon called Niger, Lucius of Cyrene, Manaen (who had been brought up with Herod the tetrarch) and Saul. 2 While they were worshiping the Lord and fasting, the Holy Spirit said, "Set apart for me Barnabas and Saul for the work to which I have called them." (NIV)*

We see these prophets banding together and ministering to the Lord. The Bible mentions "sons of the prophets" nine times in the Old Testament, referring to the prophetic schools of the time. A prophet, therefore, shouldn't be a lone ranger as much as possible; it is sanctified wisdom!

Lastly, under this point, a prophet that eats all the time is a fool—not exactly my words! Since the ministry of a prophet requires hearing from God, the stomach must be well-regulated to forestall it from getting in the way. A prophetic vessel must not be indulgent with food. I am not saying that the prophetic gift cannot flow if you are not fasting, but a prophet needs to fast for sensitivity to the Holy Spirit.

Finger 4: Don't be a performer

A prophet is expected by people to prophesy to everyone at every time. Folks often think that a prophet knows everything or can solve every of their problem. The truth, however, is that a prophet only knows what God decides to reveal to him at any time. Listen to Elisha, "...her soul is in deep distress, and the LORD has hidden it from me and has not told me (2 Kings 4: 27)."

Perhaps more than anyone else, a prophet must rely on grace as it is futile to try to earn God's gifts and anointing. Gospel ministers often go to a ridiculous extent trying to make things happen without grace. It is important to remember that God will not put answers to all the problems in anyone's life lest He makes you a god to him/her! That is why a prophet shouldn't be a lone ranger; it is wise to minister to people in the company of other ministers—we are not competing but complementing.

At the same time, we must not steal prophecies from so-called established prophets, as happened during President Joe Biden's election, where many prophets stole false prophecies from one another.

> *[30] "Therefore," declares the Lord, "I am against the prophets who steal from one another words supposedly from me. [31] Yes," declares the Lord, "I am against the prophets who wag their own tongues and yet declare, 'The Lord declares.' (Jer. 23: 30-31, NIV).*

Now a prophet only speaks for God, and he should keep quiet if God isn't talking. There is a thin line separating representing God and representing oneself. Listen to scriptures:

> *Nevertheless even among the rulers many believed in Him, but because of the Pharisees they did not confess Him, lest they should be put out of the synagogue; for they loved the praise of men more than the praise of God (John 12: 42-43, NKJV).*

How many prophets and pastors today love the praise of men more than God? Unknown to many, the vision has changed to ambition for them. God's vision for your life benefits others, but ambition benefits you. If you succumb to pressure to perform and do funny things, you are simply feathering your own nest and not that of His kingdom. Even then, only God knows the depth of what He is doing in some meetings where we may think the Spirit is not moving.

I ministered in an overnight prayer meeting (called "night vigil" in some African churches) in a church in Navan, Ireland 2003. It was one of my worst ministrations as it felt dry and as if the heavens were blocked. As I was about to return the microphone, the Lord said, "There is a woman here that I am redeeming her time; I will unwind time for her." I announced that excitedly expecting someone to hit the floor under the power, but nothing like that happened. I went home in frustration.

However, in the morning, a woman called to give her testimony: each of her three sons woke up at different times to express surprise that she looked much younger. When she finally looked in the mirror, she couldn't believe her eyes. She, in fact, called her sister in London and her husband, that was away in South Africa, to tell her story. When the husband returned home from the trip, he insisted on seeing me and the whole family came. The Bible says that "He gives seeds to the sower," meaning that we can't sow our own seeds as they must be His.

Lastly, a prophet must know his lane and stay there. Knowing what God assigns you to do and focusing on it is beautiful! Much of the competition among ministers today sprang from efforts to do what others are doing: making waves that may not be your terrain. I surely know what God is asking me to do— apart from winning souls, He has called me to release people into their birthrights and inheritance in Christ. Most of my prophetic words on people have to do with what they are doing wrong and what God wants them to do. Also, what they are suffering from, the source, and solutions to their problems. Of course, fantastic miracles are happening, but everything is tied to helping them to access God's amazing grace and power so that they can be wired up for power to be what God called them to be and to do what He wants them to do.

Finger 5: He must be Spirit-and-self-controlled

How do you feel when you have privileged information that is all-important? Again, how do you feel when you know people's secrets, their hidden problems, and divine solution to them? No doubt, the prophetic anointing is intoxicating. Listen to Elisha:

> *When Elisha the man of God heard that the king of Israel had torn his robes, he sent him this message: "Why have you torn your robes? Have the man come to me and he will know that there is a prophet in Israel (2 Kings 5: 8, NIV)."*

That is why a prophet must combine Spirit-control with self-control. When the prophets in Corinth behaved as though they were lost in the Spirit, Paul told them:

> *The spirits of prophets are subject to the control of prophets. For God is not a God of disorder but of*

> *peace—as in all the congregations of the Lord's people (1 Cor. 14: 32-33, NIV).*

This passage shows that when prophets fail to control themselves, disorderliness and tension become the result. In a culture where gospel ministers assume the pump and pageantry of Rock stars, prophets called to point the way must be above board to set good examples. A prophet, therefore, must be spiritual and disciplined in the following areas:

Unrighteous Mammon (Money)

In 2 Kings 4: 1-7, a prophet's widow petitioned Elisha because her late husband's creditors wanted to take her two sons as bondmen. The late man feared the Lord but died a pauper—a disgrace to his calling and family! The life of Job revealed that righteousness is value-added and not a liability; so, this man was not poor because he feared the Lord but because he violated some principles of prosperity and divine welfare.

Prophets today have very different challenges with money. The temptation is for them to wrest money via passive manipulations because of the grace they carry, and this is simony, as discussed above. Since money is so tempting and needs are always there, a prophet must be principled about money; a borderless life is what leads people to violations. To travel the higher road, a prophet needs a constant and rapid diagnostic appraisal of self.

I have realized that it is a snare for me to be vulnerable to peer pressure, compete with anyone, or envy anyone. Of course, a decent person must be emulative of good practices. But it is unconscionable to lend oneself to the bandwagon effects. It is a fact that we have genuine prophets today regarded as false prophets because of their spongy attitude to money. How many prophets today can reject Naaman's very generous gifts? What Elisha refused amounted to great wealth; a kind of leprosy follows the love of money, so prophets beware!

The Lord knows how to bless His children. More than what Elisha refused from Naaman, Ben-Hadad gave him:

> *Hazael went to meet Elisha, taking with him as a gift forty camel-loads of all the finest wares of Damascus. He went in and stood before him, and said, "Your son Ben-Hadad king of Aram has sent me to ask, 'Will I recover from this illness?'" (2Kings 8:9, NIV).*

If he had refused to take this gift, it would indeed have made the report, isn't it?

Profanity

A prophet must refrain from stealing the show by becoming the focus of his ministry. Anytime attention shifts from Christ the Lord to any minister, it is an abomination. We saw in the Bible how God sent John the Baptist as the forerunner of our Lord Jesus Christ. He was called to declare Jesus Christ to the nation of Israel and then get out of the way. He declared Him but getting out of the way became his problem. We saw him struggle with the Lord to his own relegation and sad exit.

The prophetic grace makes the carrier very popular, but deliberate efforts are needed by the prophet to get himself out of the way of the Lord. It is a snare when prophets tend to become replacements for the Lord in the people's lives such that they don't live by faith in Christ anymore. It is disheartening to hear believers quoting their pastors instead of the Bible. I've listened to not a few testimonies that only glorify the pastor and not our Lord Jesus Christ.

Some people are fast gaining religious notoriety. Imagine a prophet who rides on the back of a flattering testimony like: "I thank my father in the Lord for preserving my life; recently, I had an auto-accident when suddenly my pastor appeared to me and asked me to shout, "I am lifted." Immediately I found myself outside the car unhurt, but everyone else died in the car." Can you imagine that this is happening in a Pentecostal ministry? Anywhere this happens, the people cannot grow up to have a personal and dynamic relationship with the Lord but must depend on their leader as they become his customers. Obviously, that is not the purpose of the gifts of the Spirit.

Privilege Abuse

When God reveals secrets to His prophets, it is an investment of privileged information, and care must be taken not to abuse it. A prophet must be able to keep secrets from God or His people, and it is an abuse for anyone to react or look down on anyone because of secrets revealed by the Lord. I know how difficult this is. Imagine visiting a friend whose wife abuses you in her mind, and the Holy Spirit allows you to hear her mind talking? This happened to our Lord Jesus Christ often as He could perceive what people were thinking in their minds. What about people holding a meeting against you, and your spirit is with them like Elisha told Gehazi (2Kings 5:26)? Imagine if you hear the voices of people backbiting against you far away from them? All these are to protect you, and you must not use the privilege against them.

A minister of Christ is called into the ministry of reconciliation. It is not our place to be judgmental; therefore, we must reject the temptation to look down on anyone, no matter their actions. According to the Scriptures, we may have to rebuke people, but this must be done in love and humility. A prophet must learn to pray on revelations to know when and how to release them. Again, he must beware not to retrogress into controlling people; it is a temptation that must be overcome.

Opposition

Most prophets in the Bible faced opposition, and ditto for prophets today. There is no way a prophet who practices truth will not face some opposition because prophets have the ministry to point people to the right standing with God. In retrospect, while a prophet must be teachable, he must also have thick skin to insist on righteousness. This is one reason a prophet needs to be close to God in prayers, worship, and study of the word and have good company with fellow prophets.

Presumption

Elijah and his master Elisha said, "...Lord, before whom I stand..." (1 Kings 17: 1; 18: 5; 2 Kings 3: 14), and I like that. A prophet must know where he stands because it is presumptuous to act when the anointing is not flowing—of course, we also minister by faith, but we should make it clear to the people. A prophet cannot afford to rely on experience in his ministrations and work with God as you need to know how heavy His hand is on your head at different times. That is why Elijah chose to run away from Jezebel after encountering the prophets of Baal; he surely knew how tired he was because he had dissipated energy! A prophet must be watchful and discernible

CONFESSIONAL PRAYERS

Prayer of Self-Affirmation in Christ

Position

I (Put your name) am an empowered son/daughter of God (John 1: 12); I am born not of blood, nor the will of the flesh, nor the intention of man, but of God (John 1: 13).

I am one-spirit with the Lord (1 Corinthians 6:17).

I am a partaker of the divine nature and have escaped worldly corruption and lust (2 Peter 1: 4).

I am an heir of God and a Joint-Heir with Christ (Rom. 8: 17).

The Holy Spirit leads me; I am a son/daughter of God (Rom. 8: 14).

I don't belong to myself; I am bought at the price of the shed blood of Christ. My body is the Temple of the Holy Spirit; He lives in me. Therefore, I honor God with my body and sin no longer lives in me (1 Cor. 9: 18-20).

I have been crucified with Christ, and I no longer live, but Christ lives in me. The life I now live in the body, I live by the faith of the Son of God, who loved me and gave himself for me (Gal. 2: 20).

I have an anointing from the Holy One and know everything (1 John 2: 20).

I have been raised with Christ; therefore, my heart is set on things above, where Christ is, seated at the right hand of God. My mind is fixed on things above, not on earthly things. I am dead to sin and no longer a slave to it. My life is hidden with Christ in God. When Christ—who is my life, appears, I will appear with Him in glory (Col. 3: 1-4).

I am justified by the blood of Jesus Christ, who died and was raised to life; He is at the right hand of God, interceding for me. Therefore, no one can condemn me, and no one can separate me from the love of Christ. No trouble, hardship, persecution, famine, nakedness, danger, or sword! In all things, I am more than conquerors through Christ who loved me. For I am convinced that neither death nor life, neither angels nor demons, neither the present nor the future, nor any powers, neither height nor depth nor anything else in all creation, will be able to separate me from the love of God that is in Christ Jesus our Lord (Rom. 8: 34-39).

Jesus Christ is the light of the world; because I follow Him, I cannot walk in Darkness as I have the light of life (John 8: 12).

Therefore, I am the world's shining light; everywhere I go is illuminated. I am a city on the hill that cannot hide (Matt. 5: 14; Phil. 2: 15).

I am a wild olive branch cut off and grafted into God's olive tree; I share in the nourishing sap from the olive root of Abraham. Therefore, I am cut off and protected from ancestral curses and inherited liabilities (Rom. 11: 17-24).

The devil is my footstool; I tread on the lion and cobra and trample the great lion and the serpent (Ps 91: 13).

I am redeemed; I say so. It is my enemies' time to worry (Ps 107: 2).

It is fruitless to attack me; no weapon forged against me prosper, and I am a judge over every tongue that accuses me. This is my heritage and vindication as a servant of the Lord from whom my righteousness flows (Isa. 54: 17).

I am not ignorant of the devices of Satan, and he cannot take advantage of me (2 Cor. 2: 11).

It is suicidal to rise against me; I have a Savior, Shepherd, Lord, and Master—I am a most precious possession of the Almighty God and the only source of life! I lack nothing—absolutely.

My problems and challenges are dead on arrival; my enemies are regrettable entities witnessing my endowment with an ever-increasing grace and continuous celebration as the one God loves. Under their helpless watch, I revel in God's amazing love and sparkle in His lavishing, tender mercies. I flaunt God's presence as the greatest blessing and inheritance. Goodness and mercies are my escorts everywhere I live and go (Ps 23).

Blessed is the Lord who enlarges my domain! I live there like a lion, tearing off the arm, ripping open the skull. By divine authority, I take the best place; the leader's portion was reserved for me. I take my place at the head; I carry out the LORD's righteous will and His judgments in my generation. I am a young lion, springing out with zeal. Satisfied with the favor, I brim with blessings. I spill over with blessings as I take possession of land, sea, and sky (Deut. 33:20-23).

I (Put your name) am the one my brothers praise; my hand is on the neck of my enemies; my enemies bow down to me. I (Put your name) am a young lion home fresh from the kill. Like a lion, I crouch and lie down, like a lioness—who dares to provoke or rouse me? The scepter does not depart from me, or the ruler's staff from between my feet, until Shiloh, my Lord Jesus Christ, the one for whom I am holding the fort, the one to whom the obedience of the nations belongs, returns. I tether my donkey to a vine, my colt to the choice vine; I wash my garments in wine, my robes in the blood of grapes. My eyes are darker and more sparkling than wine, and my teeth are whiter than milk (Gen. 49: 8-12).

I have the message from God; I can neither be cursed nor denounced. God has blessed and accepted me; who can curse or denounce me then? From whatever viewpoint— the rocky peaks or from the heights —my demeanor is royal. Distinct, I am set apart from the nations. Who can count my blessings or number the fourth part of my inheritance in Christ? I am righteous in Christ, and today and tomorrow, I am the envy of others. The LORD lives in me and puts His Word in my mouth. This is God's oracle concerning me: "Arise, Satan, and listen; hear this, son of Darkness. God is not a man, that He should lie, nor a son of man, that He should change His mind. Does He speak and then not act? Does He promise and not fulfill? The Lord has commanded my blessings; I am blessed, and He will not repent. No misfortune is seen in me, no misery observed in my personality. The LORD, my God, is with me; the shout of the King is mine. God brought me out of sin and shame; I have the strength of a wild ox. There is no sorcery against me, no divination against my person. It will now be said of me and my personality, 'See what God has done!' I rise like a lioness; I rouse myself like a lion that does not rest till he devours his prey and drinks his victim's blood." God has blessed me, and it cannot please Him to harm me. I am the apple of His eye (Num. 23: 5-23).

I am proud of my joy-filled relationship with the Lord. I have the greatest joy possible–I hear and obey the Lord's voice perfectly. I am blessed with an abundance of visions and revelations from the Lord. I don't boast like ignorant folks devoid of spiritual revelations, boasting of money, power, and fame —things no one can take out of this world. I boast of spiritual revelations and special fellowship privileges with God. Therefore, there is no limit to the revelations of God that I can have: I will see heaven while living on earth and experience the mountain of transfiguration; I will visit heaven while on earth, in and out of the body. I will hear inexpressible and privileged conversations of heaven, things I am not permitted to tell. I will boast about things like that and not transient ecstasies from life's pleasures (2 Cor. 12: 1-5).

Blessing

I am blessed inside-out, at home, and in my journeys (Deut. 28: 6).

My children are blessed, the work of my hands is blessed, and I am ever-increasing. There is no stopping, suppressing, or reducing me (Deut. 28: 4).

I am free from the love of money; I am satisfied and contented. I cannot have less than I need because God is faithful to me. The Lord God is my all-in-all; He does not leave, forsake, or fail me. So, I say with total confidence, the Lord is my helper; I am not afraid, and there is nothing mere mortals can do to me (Heb. 13: 5-6)

All things are mine; whether the world or life or death or the present or the future—all are mine, and I am of Christ, and Christ is of God (1 Cor. 3: 22-23).

I dwell in the secret place of the Most High and abide under the shadow of the Almighty. The Lord is my refuge and fortress: my God, whom I trust. Indeed, He delivers me from the snare of the fowler and the noisome pestilence. He covers me with His feathers, and under his wings, I trust: His truth is my shield and buckler. I am not afraid of the terror by night, the arrow that flies by day, the pestilence that walks in Darkness, nor for the destruction that wastes at noonday. A thousand shall fall at my side, and ten thousand at my right hand, but it shall not come near me. I only watch and see the reward of the wicked (Psalm 91:1-8).

I am a faithful saint in Christ. I have grace and peace from God our Father and the Lord Jesus Christ. I am blessed with every spiritual blessing in the heavenly places in Christ. I am chosen in Christ before the world's creation to be holy and blameless in His sight. In love, He predestined me to be adopted as His son/daughter through Jesus Christ by His pleasure and will. I am the specimen of His glorious grace and the evident beauty of His praise in Christ. I am redeemed through His blood and totally forgiven of all my sins by the riches of God's grace that He lavished on me with all wisdom and understanding. I know the mystery of His will according to His good pleasure, which He purposed in Christ. I am chosen in Christ and predestined to conform to God's purpose and perfect will; therefore, I am for the praise of His glory. I am included in Christ through faith in Him; I believed and am marked in Christ with a seal, the promised Holy Spirit, a deposit guaranteeing my inheritance until the redemption of those who are God's possession—to the praise of His glory.

For this reason, I give thanks to God non-stop in gratitude and worship. I have the Spirit of wisdom and revelation in my knowledge of God. The eyes of my heart are enlightened; therefore, I know the hope to which He has called me, the riches of His glorious inheritance in the saints, and His incomparably great power for me who believe. That power is like the working of His mighty strength, which he performed in Christ, when he raised him from the dead and set him at his own right hand in the heavenly places, Far above all principality, and power, and might, and dominion, and every name that is named, not only in this age, but also in that which is to come: And has put all things under his feet, and gave him to be the head over all things to the church, Which is his body, the fullness of him that fills all in all (Eph. 1: 1-22).

I'm amazed at what great love the Father has lavished on me that I should be called a child of God! And that is what I am! The world does not know me because it did not know Him. Praise the Lord, I am a child of God, and what I will be has not yet been known. But I know that when Christ appears, I shall be like Him, for I shall see Him as He is. I have this hope in me; therefore, I purify myself, just as He is pure (1 John 3: 1-2).

Duty

I am the kind of worshiper the Father seeks and finds. God is Spirit, and I worship Him in the Spirit and truth (John 4: 23-24).

My eyes are fixed on the Lord Jesus Christ, the Author and Finisher of my faith (Heb. 12: 2).

The Holy Spirit is resident in me; I am empowered to be a witness for Christ worldwide and demonstrate that Jesus Christ is Lord (Acts 1: 8).

I have power and authority over all demons and to cure diseases. I am sent—by the Lord Jesus Christ to preach God's kingdom and heal the sick (Luke 9:1-2).

I can do all things through Christ who strengthens me (Philippians 4:13).

I believe in Christ—therefore, all things are possible to me (Mark 9:23).

I have the peace of God; I am sent by the Lord Jesus Christ, just like His Father sent Him—forgiving sins and retaining some by the Spirit of God (John 20:21-23).

I am commanded to go and teach the Gospel of Christ with the full backing of all authority in heaven and on earth; the Lord is always with me to the very end of the age (Matthew 28:18-20).

I did not choose myself; Jesus Christ appointed me to run with the Gospel and bear the fruit that endures. Therefore, whatever I ask in the name of Christ, the Father gives me (John 15: 16).

Most assuredly, I believe in Jesus Christ; therefore, the works that He did are precisely what I am doing. Further, I am doing "Greater works" because He's returned to His Father, and I hold the fort. Whatever I ask in His name is what He does to the glory of the Father in the Son (John 14: 12-13).

The Spirit of the Sovereign Lord is on me because the Lord has anointed me to proclaim good news to the poor. He has sent me to bind up the brokenhearted, to proclaim freedom for the captives and release from Darkness for the prisoners, to proclaim the year of the Lord's favor and the day of vengeance of our God, to comfort all who mourn, and provide for those who grieve in Zion—to bestow on them a crown of beauty instead of ashes, the oil of joy instead of mourning, and a garment of praise instead of a spirit of despair. They will be called oaks of righteousness, a planting of the Lord to display his splendor (Isa. 61: 1-3).

Therefore, I am standing on my feet because Christ has appeared to me for His purpose that is higher than me, to appoint me as a minister and a witness of what I have seen and will be revealed to me. My rescue from persecution is guaranteed! He has sent me to open their eyes and turn them from Darkness to light and from the power of Satan to God so that they may receive forgiveness of sins and an inheritance among those sanctified by faith in Christ (Acts 26: 16-18).

God has anointed me in Jesus of Nazareth with the Holy Spirit, and with power, I go about, doing good and healing all who are oppressed by the devil, for God is with me (Acts 10: 38).

I am in the hands of God and am committed to the word of His grace, which is building me up and has given me an inheritance among all sanctified (Acts 20: 32).

I love the Lord; circumstances and situations bow to His grace in my life, and nothing can negate my inheritance in Christ. I am called according to His purpose; therefore, He causes all things to work together for my good (Rom. 8: 28).

Like Jesus, like me, His son/daughter, everything is written about me in the Holy Scriptures; every promise and every blessing shall be fulfilled (Luke 18: 31).

Those who would ensnare me fall into their pits and

hang on their stakes (Pro. 26: 27).

There is no wisdom, no insight, no plan that can succeed against the Lord (Pro 21: 30).

Therefore, nothing on earth or in heaven can annul the Word of God in my life. I call into judgment every person, Spirit or flesh, who is angry about God's grace on my life, who fights God's blessing on my life, or who is displeased with God's tender mercies that I enjoy.

Issue out your judgment here.

(Culled from acts1038.com)

Confession of Obedience to the Lord's Call

I imbibe the admonition given to Archippus; I will carefully fulfill the ministry I received in the Lord (Colossians 4:17).

I will always follow the right path and stay within it. I refuse to follow in the footsteps of Balaam, the son of Beor, who loved money and was punished for his iniquity. A dumb donkey, speaking with a human voice, stopped the mad prophet from committing a sinful act. I am not dumb spiritually, but discernible and will not be rebuked for my actions (2 Peter 2:15-16).

Despite being an unbeliever, Nebuchadnezzar, the king of Babylon, was called "My servant" by the Lord—a reminder that the Lord can use anyone to serve His purpose. As a child of God, I trust that Nebuchadnezzar will not rebuke me (Jeremiah 27:6-8).

The LORD refers to Cyrus as His chosen one. He held his right hand to conquer nations, strip kings of their armor, and open the double doors before him so the gates would not be shut. "For the sake of my servant Jacob and Israel My chosen one, I have even called you by your name, I have named you, though you have not known Me. I am the LORD, and there is no other; There is no God besides Me. I will gird you, though you have not known Me, [6] That they may know from the rising of the sun to its setting That there is none besides Me. I am the LORD, and there is no other," He said. I am better than Cyrus because I know the Lord and worship Him. I will serve the Lord wholeheartedly, so Cyrus will not rebuke me (Isaiah 45:1,4-6).

Prophet Micaiah saw the LORD sitting on His throne and all the hosts of heaven standing by, on His right and left. He heard the LORD say, 'Who will persuade Ahab to go up, that he may fall at Ramoth Gilead?' He saw an unclean spirit volunteer and commissioned to be a lying spirit in the mouth of all Ahab's prophets and prevail. Therefore, I will neither hesitate nor fail to serve the Lord enthusiastically and faithfully. No demon will be more obedient to the Lord than me (1 Kings 22:19-23).

I am a golden vessel of honor in the Lord's great house. I have cleansed myself of iniquity; therefore, I am a vessel of honor, sanctified and useful for the Master, prepared for every good work (2 Timothy 2:20-21).

I cannot take this honor to myself, but I am called by God, just as Aaron was (Hebrews 5:4). Like Apostle Paul, I am not disobedient to the heavenly vision and calling (Acts 26:19). Like Paul, whatever were gains to me I now consider loss for the sake of Christ. What is more, I consider everything a loss because of the surpassing worth of knowing Christ Jesus, my Lord, for whose sake I am ready even to lose all things if required of the Lord. I consider them garbage, that I may gain Christ, and be found in him, not having a legalistic self-righteousness, but gift-righteousness through faith in Christ—the righteousness endowed by God based on faith (Philippians 3:7-9).

Like Moses, I refuse by faith to hang on to my earthly heritage, percussions, benefits, or opportunities. I choose to identify with the Gospel of Christ and the cross it stands for rather than to enjoy the fleeting pleasures of sin. I esteem the reproach of Christ as greater riches than the treasures in the world, looking to the reward (Hebrews 11:24-26).

God testified concerning David: 'I have found David, son of Jesse, a man after my own heart; he will do everything I want him to do.' David is dead, and God can no longer use him. I am today's David and am after God's heart. I will do everything God requires of me without fail or error. Like David, I will serve God's purpose before my race is run and I see the Lord (Acts 13:22,36).

Therefore, I am encouraged by the Lord, like Jeremiah. I am not too young or old to serve God's purpose. I must and will go to everyone He sends me to and say whatever He commands me. I am not afraid of anyone because the Lord is with me and will rescue me. The Lord has touched my mouth and put His Words in my mouth. In Christ, He has appointed me over nations and kingdoms to uproot, tear down, destroy, overthrow, build, and plant. The Word of the LORD comes to me, and I see correctly; He ensures His Word is fulfilled. I am red alert to declare the pure Word of the Lord. I am not terrified by anyone lest God terrify me before them. The Lord has made me a fortified city, an iron pillar, and a bronze wall to stand against the whole kingdom of Satan--its principalities, powers, the rulers of the darkness of this age, and spiritual hosts of wickedness in the heavenly places. It is suicidal of them to fight against me because the Sovereign LORD is with me and protecting me (Jeremiah 1:7-13,17-19).

Because the Sovereign LORD helps me, I will not be disgraced. Therefore, I have set my face like flint, and I know I will not be put to shame. He who vindicates me is near. Who then will bring charges against me? Let us face each other! Who is my accuser? Let him confront me! It is the Sovereign LORD who helps me. Who will condemn me? They will all wear out like a garment; the moths will eat them up (Jeremiah 1:7-13,17-19)

I know those who hate God will not listen to me because they are impudent and hard-hearted. I know the Lord has made my face strong against their faces and my forehead strong against their foreheads. God has made my forehead like adamant stone, harder than flint; I am not afraid of them, nor dismayed at their looks, though they are rebellious and dangerous (Ezekiel 3:7-9).

1 I don't lift up my eyes except unto the Lord.

2 My help comes from the LORD, who made heaven and earth.

3 He does not let my foot slip — He who watches over me does not slumber;

4 indeed, He who watches over me neither slumber nor sleep.

5 The LORD watches over me — the LORD is my shade at my right hand;

6 the sun will not harm me by day, nor the moon by night.

7 The LORD keeps me from all harm — He watches over my life;

8 the LORD watches over my coming and going both now and for evermore (Ps 121).

1 Because I trust in the LORD, I am like Mount Zion, which cannot be shaken but endures forever.

2 As the mountains surround Jerusalem, so the LORD surrounds me His own both now and for evermore.

3 The scepter of the wicked does not remain over the land allotted to me; I shall not use my hands to do evil.

4 I am good and upright in heart, and the Lord is good to me.

5 But those who turn to crooked ways the LORD will banish with the evildoers; but peace shall be upon me (Ps 125).

1 I dwell in the shelter of the Most High and therefore rest in the shadow of the Almighty.

2 I say of the LORD, "He is my refuge and my fortress, my God, in whom I trust."

3 Surely, He saves me from the fowler's snare and from the deadly pestilence.

4 He covers me with his feathers, and under his wings I find refuge; his faith- fulness is my shield and rampart.

5 I don't fear the terror of night, nor the arrow that flies by day.

6 Nor for the pestilence that walks in dark- ness; nor for the destruction that wastes at noonday.

7 A thousand may fall at my side, ten thou- sand at my right hand, but it will not come near me.

8 I will only observe with my eyes and see the punishment of the wicked.

9 Because I have made the Most High my dwelling — even the LORD, who is my refuge —

10 therefore, no harm befalls me, no disaster comes near my tent.

11 For God has commanded His angels concerning me to guard me in all my ways;

12 they lift me up in their hands, and I don't strike my foot against a stone.

13 I tread upon the lion and the cobra; I trample the great lion and the serpent.

14 "Because (Put your name) loves me," says the LORD, "I will rescue him/her; I will protect him/her, for he/she acknowledges my name.

15 He/she will call upon me, and I will answer him/her; I will be with him/her in trouble, I will deliver him/her and honor him/her.

16 With long life will I satisfy him/her and show him/her my salvation." (Ps 91)

RABBONI BIBLE SCHOOL

Perhaps you have noticed a negative shift in the church today: teachings are motivational and not doctrinal. Ministrations are engaging, scientific, sophisticated and entertaining but lack power of God and eternity values. Born-Again churches have abandoned the whys for hows; to the point that it is difficult to identify the so-called Evangelical, Pentecostal and Charismatic churches today based on doctrines. The End-Time churches are sociological and not theological. Believers today like to quote the catch phrases of their pastors rather than the Holy Word of God; again, most Christians nowadays know little or nothing about "The blessed hope" of our Lord's return or the coming millennium of Christ's rule or in fact, God's future plan for His kingdom. The resultant effect of this is that there is a widening gap between the Word of God and church practices today.

However, our Bible school is not programmed to correct these anomalies but to help you discover Biblical truth. We believe that fakery is mutational but truth is constant. Since there are numerous fakery and different strains of falsehood; the only sure way of identifying lies is to know truth very well.

Our curriculum is made up of simple topics that sum up compulsory knowledge of the Word of God. Each course is given out as a research to the students on which a paper must be written and debated in turn. At the end of the course, a Believer would be able to explain the Word of God "wholistically" and in depth while the Minister would be versatile in the work of the ministry, in building Believers and make them relevant to society for the uplift of our Lord Jesus

Christ alone. The school thrives on the leading of the Holy Spirit, hybridization and cross-fertilization of renewed minds as well as fellowship with the people of God; therefore, it cherishes feedbacks from its graduates for a lifetime relationship.

The projectile and course duration of each student differs as the school allows for individual speed and availability; however, normal duration is one year. To remain in school, each student must complete, at least one course per month. You can do this course online or through attendance which is not restricted to one place.

For more information and enrolment please, write:tell@acts1038.com

OTHER BOOKS BY THE AUTHOR

Confessional Prayer Bible

Imagine a Bible that doubles as a comprehensive prayer book where you pray all of God's blessings & promises straight up as you read your Holy Bible. Imagine turning the whole Bible into your own personal story, where all the blessings, promises, prayers, lessons & prophecies are personalized. Also, imagine a Holy Bible that assists you to relate to every chapter of the Bible whether it is historical, prophetic or doctrinal. That is exactly what The Confessional Prayer Bible is!

Finally, you have no excuse that:

- you don't know how to pray or

- you find it difficult to pray or

- the Holy Bible is difficult to understand or

- you find it boring or can't relate to it.

The Confessional Prayer Bible is "Wholistic" scriptures personalized: all the blessings, promises, heritage, lessons and good examples prayed into your life! It helps you to confess the word of God into your life straight up as you read it and shows you who you truly are in Christ. THE ONLY BIBLE OF ITS KIND!

The Hate Mirage

The central theme of the Holy Bible is the love of God for all mankind, and what to do with it under the free will He has gifted us. The main issue is that love goes with responsibility, without which it is not defined. Secondly, someone will not create the universe without purpose or governance. Humanity, however, hates two words, "Don't" and "Wait." This book examines biblical don'ts on our sexuality which are out of love, never hatred, to keep us in His purpose.

Further, Jesus demanded that His followers deny themselves and carry their cross daily (Luke 9: 23). This book is, therefore, written for those who believe in the Lord and submit to His Word. It is not anti-LGBTQIA; it is written to Believers to educate and remind them that God's restrictions only make sense for those who submit to Him and believe His words. It defends the Holy Bible against the barrages of attacks that it is a hate book, homophobic, archaic, and unfit for modern life and behaviors. It exposes age-long hypocrisy and apostasy in the Church, culminating in open sexual indulgences and outright rebellion against the Lord.

Blessings and Curses

You are either blessed or cursed! Curses and blessings are powerful forces in the world today and this is beyond myth. For example, generational sicknesses are encoded in the genes and Medical Doctors seem to know this and ask whether a sickness runs in the family. Rev. Baba-Lola lists different types of curses, their venom and how to lift them. He wrote that blessings are opposite of curses and are controlled by similar principles.

Let Me Run, A Call to Missions

It has taken over 2000 years of daring mission endeavors to evangelize the world but the job is not yet done. In this book, Rev. Emmanuel Baba-Lola shows that the Church is far more equipped than the task. Why then is the world not evangelized? What is the limiting factor? Surely, we need to change strategies because at the current rate, it will take about another one thousand years to complete world evangelization. What are the things we must change? You need to read this classic on the world missions and evangelization

Missions without Tears

There are different types of suffering: suffering as a fool, an ignorant, lawbreaker and for one's politico-ideology. Others are: Suffering for Christ, suffering under a curse, and suffering from religiosity. Suffering for Christ simply means persecutions, and is not synonymous with poverty, and all other forms of suffering that at times bedevil human existence and mission work. The Missions without Tears is about freedom from all creative suffering, to hasten world evangelism.

Divorce and Remarriage

Divorce and remarriage is one of the hottest topics that divide the church and yet it has become a recurring decimal even among the Evangelicals. In the West, Christian marriage has been trivialized to its elastic limit while in Africa Churches, leaders are often highhanded, at times, to ridiculous and ungodly extent. In this work, Emmanuel Baba-Lola bluntly and carefully enumerated misconceptions about Biblical marriage and concluded that God hates divorce. Period. However, God did not forbid divorce while Scriptures show the responsibilities of

Church Elders in determining the possibilities of remarriage based on individual merit.

Marriage, Point Blank

Since the 1980s, marriage has been facing incessant barrages worldwide due to Satan's efforts to destroy human discipline, ever-increasingly liberal society ethics, women subjugation, Church hypocrisy, porn, Hollywood, TV, etc. The New Testament's teachings on Marriage is very protective of all the players--husband, wife and children but over the centuries, these had always been seen through the prism of male domination and culture; the refraction has done not a few damages. In this book, Rev. Emmanuel Baba-Lola wrote that Marriage is blissful if we follow its creator's manual. He concludes that every problem bedeviling homes today is tantamount to abuse of how marriage works and its purpose. He lists the four pillars of holy matrimony in the Holy Bible and gave Biblical insights to the secrets of successful marriage.

Praying the Mind of God

To a Christian, praying to God is not an option as there can be no relationship with God if you don't talk to Him. Perhaps many Christians are praying today than ever and some are fast becoming praying machines. However, many prayers are obviously not being answered because we are more religious than spiritual on the subject of prayer. Rev. Baba-Lola shows us that a prayer is a dialogue and not monologues; he enumerated the ingredients of answered prayers and the danger of permissive will of God in anyone's life. Further, he shows us when to pray and when to take authority. He concluded that prayers are sweetest, smoothest and most rewarding when we pray the mind of God.

ABOUT THE AUTHOR

Emmanuel Baba-Lola is sent to win souls and release Believers into their birthrights and inheritance in Christ. An Alumnus of Youth With A Mission (YWAM), Jamaica, WI, missions and world evangelization have been his life passion. Apart from Shepherding New Wine Assembly, Lagos, Nigeria for about four years purposely to reach out to the neglected people groups of Lagos, he is the President of Missions Aid Network, an umbrella organization that networks God's resources for the advancement of the gospel of Christ. He convenes the Prophetic Prayer Conferences (PPC) worldwide; a prophetic atmosphere where Prophets and the people gather to worship God and connect God's grace and tender mercies. He runs Faith Clinic, a house of refuge where people go for prophetic ministries, individual prayers, deliverance, healing, and miracle services. He is the Director of Acts1038, his itinerant ministries under which he has taken the gospel of Christ to all the Continents of the world. He is the Rector of Rabboni Bible Schools and General Editor of the Confessional Prayer Bible & Rabboni Magazine, and author of seven religious literatures including Prophets & Their Burdens. His weekly Faith Clinic is a workshop where he trains people to express the grace & power of God on earth. He holds BSc. (Honors) in Agricultural Engineering. He is married to Grace, and they are blessed with four children.

www.ingramcontent.com/pod-product-compliance
Lightning Source LLC
LaVergne TN
LVHW021353080426
835508LV00020B/2270